England History

An Enthralling Overview of the English Middle Ages

(Tracing the Crossroads of Cultures and Conflicts From the Celts to the Modern Era)

Robert Steed

Published By **Bella Frost**

Robert Steed

All Rights Reserved

England History: An Enthralling Overview of the English Middle Ages (Tracing the Crossroads of Cultures and Conflicts From the Celts to the Modern Era)

ISBN 978-0-9948647-5-8

No part of this guidebook shall be reproduced in any form without permission in writing from the publisher except in the case of brief quotations embodied in critical articles or reviews.

Legal & Disclaimer

The information contained in this book is not designed to replace or take the place of any form of medicine or professional medical advice. The information in this book has been provided for educational & entertainment purposes only.

The information contained in this book has been compiled from sources deemed reliable, and it is accurate to the best of the Author's knowledge; however, the Author cannot guarantee its accuracy and validity and cannot be held liable for any errors or omissions. Changes are periodically made to this book. You must consult your doctor or get professional medical advice before using any of the suggested remedies, techniques, or information in this book.

Upon using the information contained in this book, you agree to hold harmless the Author from and against any damages, costs, and expenses, including any legal fees potentially resulting from the application of any of the information provided by this guide. This disclaimer applies to any damages or injury caused by the use and application, whether directly or indirectly, of any advice or information presented, whether for breach of contract, tort, negligence, personal injury, criminal intent, or under any other cause of action.

You agree to accept all risks of using the information presented inside this book. You need to consult a professional medical practitioner in order to ensure you are both able and healthy enough to participate in this program.

Table Of Contents

Chapter 1: Ancient Influences And Ancestors (C. 600 Bce To 1066 Ce) 1

Chapter 2: French Foreigners To Essential Englishmen (1066-1453) 15

Chapter 3: Thorns And Roses (1455-1603) 28

Chapter 4: A Roiling Crucible Of Revolution And Reform (1603-1801) 41

Chapter 5: The Empire's Ascendency And Apex (1801-1918) 58

Chapter 6: Battles, Blood, And The Death Of Imperialism (1914-Present Day) 67

Chapter 7: England's Prehistory - The First Inhabitants 83

Chapter 8: The Roman Invasion And Its Legacy 92

Chapter 9: The Anglo-Saxon Period - The Birth Of England 100

Chapter 10: The Norman Invasion - What It Meant For England................................ 116

Chapter 11: The Middle Ages In England 123

Chapter 12: The 17th And 18th Centuries In England 133

Chapter 13: The 19th And 20th Centuries In The History Of England - Key Events That Left A Mark 142

Chapter 14: England Travel - Tips For A Worthwhile Experience......................... 152

Chapter 15: The Rise And Fall Of Roman Britain 161

Chapter 1: Ancient Influences And Ancestors (C. 600 Bce To 1066 Ce)

Prior to the Romans as well as before the Romans, Angles and the Angles, Saxons and the Jutes and the Vikings along with the Normans There were other, earlier resident of England's shores. The loosely related tribe that grew from Central Europe known as the Celts were found throughout the continent, and even in the British Isles. The Celts were a part of England are referred to as Britons used the Celtic dialect, Common Brittonic, which is like Welsh as well as Gaelic. While there are evidences of an ancestral and indigenous agricultural culture in the Neolithic period--and they are believed to be the first people that built Stonehenge, but not much is understood about the peoples who lived in the area, even however their ancestors were likely to be absorbed by the Celtic civilization when it spread across the islands. Since they were a part of the Iron Age civilization, the Britons used the plow made of iron to the soil and developed distinctive square fields, which are still able to be observed to this time. They were reputedly fierce and feared The majority of information learned about the Britons originates from other sources as do the Romans who believed in their Celtic peoples from Europe as a threat that needed to be controlled. While they're now viewed as a group however, they were in reality Britons comprised a mix of diverse tribes. it was their inability to join forces that caused being the subject of Roman control of England and brought the end of Celtic rule in the region through their victory over Claudius the Emperor. Claudius in 43 CE.

Also known in the form of Britannia to the Romans The land was previously been attacked in the reign of Julius Caesar around 55 BCE before it was placed in the hands of Roman control a hundred years after. The Romans took their legions, language as well as their laws to England as they sought to extend their authority to Wales as well as Scotland as well, which was known to their fellow Romans in the form of Cambria and Caledonia and Caledonia, respectively. Even though Roman legions were able to make an effort to expand to Wales but it was not subject to the similar Romanization as seen in east. Scotland was, on the contrary side, was a different matter completely. It was the place where Romans were pushing towards the north, fighting the Celtic Caledonians until their defeat in the hands of Julius Agricola around 81 CE However, the Caledonians were a constant thorn in the side of Romans always threatening the northernmost parts of the Roman Empire. In 117 CE, eventually the

Hadrian, the Emperor of Rome Hadrian constructed a wall in the area of today's border that separates England and Scotland to regulate the flow of individuals within and out of the area and also to distinguish those living in Roman settlements from those he deemed to be "barbarians." The Caledonians continued to pose a threat always pinning down and destroying Hadrian's Wall when it was necessary that the Roman army was sent in other parts in the empire. After the conclusion of the Roman period, these inhabitants were called the Picts as well as the Scots.

In the midst that of Roman invading England Icenis, a group of Britons named Icenis in the eastern region of England (known in later times in the future as East Anglia) was ruled by a fierce, red-haired queen called Boudicca. Following the demise of her husband, her estate was taken by Roman soldiers. Her daughters were sexually assaulted, and she was brutally beaten publicly while a large portion of her Iceni tribe members were taken captive. In fury, she led Iceni Iceni along with other Celtic tribes to revolt and sacked London as well as St. Albans (known then as Londinium and Verulamium). Then, eventually they were defeated by the Romans beat the Britons in battle, and Boudicca was believed to have slain her life in order to escape Roman capture.

After the division of Boudicca and her adherents, England under the Romans was relatively tranquil, and the roads that they built has a long-lasting impact on the manner in which the nation would be developed and settled for the foreseeable future. The cities in York, Bath, and Lincoln were founded all during Roman administration, and the numerous military roads that they constructed for connecting these towns to the harbors in London continue to be connected through their systems up to the present. England was a major beneficiary of the immense size that was the Roman Empire which allowed them to expand their trade market and to come in contact with luxurious goods imported from far countries. Even though the Romans were invading the land but maintained a substantial army presence in order to protect the nearby Celtic tribes but they didn't replace the population of the area. Instead, the higher classes who existed prior to the Roman invasion had simply took on Roman methods to dress, live, and even speaking. Meanwhile, the less privileged classes continued to function the same way they had always done in the past, squeezing a decent living out of the ground under their foot.

In the end, when Rome began to decay within, their grip over Britain was weakened. Caledonians constantly smashed away near the northern boundary and groups of Saxons originated from Central Germany, initially brought into the islands to fight off the invasions of Scotland and Ireland started to plunder throughout the western and southern coasts of Britain. When the western portion of the Roman Empire finally crumbled in 476 CE, the romanized Britons were in their own for a long while and were already under the sway of the newly-arrived Anglo-Saxons. Rome was able to connect to the British Isles to the rest of mainland Europe by way of trade and commerce which would remain crucial to the long-term future of the country of England. The Romans brought Latin along, which was being one of the greatest predecessors of that English language. However, besides the ruin they of their legacy and the road they constructed, Rome left England with an ideology that shaped society throughout the centuries. Even as Roman influence diminished, Christianity remained an enduring tradition.

Central as well as Western Germanic tribes known as the Angles, Saxons, Jutes and Frisians were utilized during throughout the Roman Empire to defend Britannia against the Caledonians as well as Irish tribes. But now without the legions they had begun to establish themselves in England. They were viewed by the Romano-British community as an outsider, and opposed by Celtic tribes from Wales and Scotland and Wales, the Germanic tribes initially were met by hostile reactions. At this point the myth of King Arthur was created, featuring Arthur being a leader of the Romano-Briton tribe in opposition to the new invaders. They were however, violent people, and the defenseless and Romanized Britons didn't pose any threat. There is a need to note that very little writing exists from the time of this which means it can't be proven with absolute certainty the amount of brutality that the Angles and Saxons committed against the Britons and how many Britons just allowed themselves to accept the new society, just as they did with the Romans prior to their time. In any case, as people of the Anglo-Saxon community spread and spread, they introduced their Old English language to England and the Germanic foundation that is the basis of modern English is due. The monarchical government they had along with a form of proto-parliament referred to as the Witan created the basis to the present Constitutional monarchy and Parliament. In addition, many of the names used for cities and regions within England have their roots in the Anglo-Saxons. For instance, although the Romans have called the area Britannia but it was soon given the designation "Land of the Angles" which later was shortened to England.

In around 650 CE, seven anglo-Saxon kingdoms were founded: Essex, Sussex, Wessex, East Anglia, Mercia, Northumbria, and Kent. In the following 200 years the seven kingdoms would be merged into three: Wessex Mercia Northumbria, and Wessex--with Mercia being the biggest and most influential before the early 800s CE. While Mercia was the biggest landmass and historically was the most powerful in terms of political power however, the Royal Windsor family in the 21st century is not able to trace its roots back to old rulers from Mercia. The honor of Mercia is held by the ruling family of Wessex. In the time that the formidable ruler Ecbert of Wessex became king during the first 800 years CE He subdued Mercia and laid the foundation for the fusion of Mercia as well as Wessex with his son, Alfred the Great, who was referred to as the King of English. The final fusion of Wessex, Mercia, and Northumbria into England was achieved under the first King of England and Ecbert's great-great-grandson, Aethelstan.

As the Anglo-Saxon community began to develop, settle and grow throughout the 700s CE but a new wave of trespassers who were armed with guns started to take notice of the increasing prosperity. The natives from Scandinavia and referred to by Anglo-Saxons under the names of the Danes as well as the Norse or Northmen, Vikings descended on the British Isles in the late 700s C.E. Starting with the initial raids and pillaging, during the time of Alfred the Great during the early 800s the attacks were transformed to permanent camps. Following numerous bitter battles against Viking troops, Alfred withdrew to the Somerset Marshes to regroup before triumphantly defeating the Vikings during the Battle of Edington in 878 CE. Alfred knew that Viking settlements were not sufficiently secure and his own resources diminished to remove them completely from England He therefore concluded an agreement with their king, Guthrum. This resulted in a unique region in Northern as well as Eastern England known as the Danelaw which meant that the Viking settlements could continue to live peacefully together with the Anglo-Saxons.

However, it was not enough to stop the Viking threat. The fighting and raids continued until the 9th century. England was even home to four Scandinavian rulers when Sweyn forkbeard was crowned King of England by his fellow Saxon leader, Aethelred II the Unready. The most effective of the four foreign rulers is the King Cnut who had the vast kingdom of England, Denmark, Norway and even a part of Sweden. The kingdom was only a short time in existence as his sons Harthacnut and Harold could not control the throne of his North Sea Empire after his passing away. The English the throne was restored from Harthacnut's Saxon half-brother, and Aethelred II, the son of Aethelred, Edward the Confessor.

Although the Anglo-Saxon line was restored to the throne Edward lived the bulk of his existence living in exile over the English Channel in Normandy. The Normandy king had no friends within England and relied on the backing of noblemen and, in particular, his future spouse's family known as the Godwins in order to ensure the rule of his family. The moment Edward lost his child in the year 1066 CE, three weak claimants to the English the throne were in place, causing the country into chaos and confusion. The first one was Harold Godwinson, who, even though he was not of any royal blood, was uncle of the monarch and also a brother to the queen. The other is Edgar Aetheling, the late great-grandson of the late king, who had the highest blood lineage, yet not enough political capital to support it. The third one was William his father, Duke of Normandy and a cousin of the late King; his bloodline was a major factor in his candidature However, his status as a foreign national led to his claim being questioned and slightly unappealing.

Chapter 2: French Foreigners To Essential Englishmen (1066-1453)

In England, Harold claimed that Edward the Confessor had ordained his name as the legitimate succession to the throne being aware of the many claims on the crown to the crown, he swiftly taken to the throne. In the aftermath, two factions started to accumulate and moved toward England. One was led by Tostig, Harold's brother who was exiled Tostig and The King of Norway, Harold Hardrada, eager to establish a position within England. The other was William Duke of Normandy angry at Harold's claims as a king. William's family was sheltered by Edward the Confessor throughout his exile in Normandy and claimed Edward was the one who had proclaimed William and not Harold to succeed him a few years prior to his demise. Thus, the newly-minted the King Harold of England headed north to join his brothers' forces while William of Normandy began to prepare his troops.

King Harold won the battle against the combined forces that included Tostig as well as Harold Hardrada in Stamford Bridge, but a couple of weeks later, when he rode south in order to meet the Normans the tides were turning. In a field just outside the village of Hastings, Harold and William's army fought a fierce battle. Harold passed away on the battlefield and later in 1066, October triumphant in the Battle of Hastings, William of Normandy was William the Conqueror the first Norman King of England.

Another time, a brand new cultural and language was beginning to take over England. The Normans were french-speaking Christians who had Frankish and Scandinavian roots. As of 1072 in 1072, the Normans held the power-swapping levers replacing the Anglo-Saxon nobles as well as government officials by appointing the Normans' own appointed officials. The newly-elected ruling class of England was French as well, and for the years following the reign of King Edward II, monarchs from England did not speak English. Because of this, a lot of phrases that are used in the English spoken language that refer to the laws and government such as justice, liberty and the word "people" are of French roots. In addition, the notion of primogeniture, which states that the son born first could be the heir to the crown was introduced during the Norman invasion. In Anglo-Saxon rule, although it was commonplace to have the son of the first born become the next King however, this was not a guarantee. The Witan was the only one who controlled succession to the throne choosing a king out of suitable candidates from bloodline royal.

The Normans brought ideas of architecture from mainland Europe to the islands, replacing traditional Saxon wooden structures with gothic cathedrals that soared from stone. The stunning cathedrals, castles and monasteries which dot the land of England were the consequence of the importation of Norman style of architecture. William himself was extremely organized and commissioned a major survey in 1085 that accurately assessed the riches of his kingdom. The results of the survey were then collected into the Domesday Book, which gives readers a fascinating insight into how land was divided and utilized and who was in charge of what and the way disputes were resolved.

After William passed away, he split his estate between his sons. However, his youngest son Henry I would reunite Normandy as well as England under his stewardship until 1106. But Henry I's son and heir would pass away in a drunken boat crash on the English Channel which would open the route to his daughter Matilda and her husband Geoffrey Plantagenet to lay claim to the English the throne.

THE RISE OF THE PLANTAGENETS

However, despite Matilda as well as Geoffrey's efforts, they couple never officially ruled as King and Queen of England. Their son Henry II, who took over the throne along with his queen Eleanor of Aquitaine who was the official founder of the Plantagenet Dynasty, ruling over the entirety of England in addition to vast swaths of France. The Plantagenets are also known as the Angevins for their ancestral home of Anjou they were French from the beginning as were the Norman monarchs prior to their time, they spoke primarily French during their early years.

This family's roots and claim to vast areas of France could be the basis of the seemingly endless struggle between English and French monarchs to control the region and also the basis of the long-running conflict between France and England.

The Plantagenets were an ruthless and bloody clan, often changing sides whenever they felt the situation was right for them. The husband would be a shrewd ally to his wife, brother and sister as well as fathers against his son. The Angevin Kingdom's borders were always changing as was the often-vilified King John who was the brother of Henry II and losing the bulk of French territories. Following his inability abroad, John began to levy taxation on English nobles in order to help the burden of the Royal Treasury. As a response, aided from the Archbishop Canterbury Barons of power revolted in

1215 and demanded the end of all inhumane abuses by the power of the monarchy. John who was surrounded by nobles, was forced other than to bow to the demands of their brethren, which led to the signature of the Magna Carta in June of that same year. It was the Magna Carta laid out the rights of the barons in addition to ensuring the rights of the church which effectively ended the prospect of an absolute monarchy in England. While it was true that the Magna Carta was not upheld on the surface but in the longer term it established the base to the Constitution of England and foreshadowed the skepticism that of the English will have for dictatorial rulers of the future.

As well as the tense relations over the Channel in the Channel with France, England began to claim its authority over the entire island. The King Edward I was the Longshanks introduced Wales into English control by implementing the Statute of Wales in 1284 And when his second son, Edward was born in Wales, Edward I proudly designated the son of his Prince of Wales which is held by the very first prince of England up to today. If Scotland was facing a succession crisis, Edward I seized the occasion and embarked on a long battle to get Scotland under his control. Because of his brutal battles in northern Scotland, Edward I also earned the title "The Hammer of the Scots." But Edward I and his son did not succeed in bringing Scotland into the fold and Scotland remained out of England's reach until the time of the Stuart monarchs of the 15th century.

In the distance, across the turbulent waters that separated England and France and the king of France, Charles IV died without a successor in 1328. Then the King

Edward III of England laid claim to the French the throne as his mother was Charles IV's daughter. Edward III's army were in France in 1339 and began the long and brutal battle between the two nations known by the name of the Hundred Years' War (1337-1453). In the beginning, Edward III had resounding victories, his troops and those of his son, the Black Prince, winning at the Battles for Crecy (1346) as well as Poitiers (1356) in turn. The next 20 years however, the French started to pull back. By 1375, the Treaty of Bruges in 1375 nearly all of Edward III's victories vanished and he left England in the middle of Calais and a narrow strip of coast in Southern France. The losses he suffered in France caused discontent from the inside, while the Bubonic disease ravaged the countryside in the 1375-year period, destroying a large portion of the population as well as causing economic and social difficulties.

Unrest among the peasantry was growing following the death of Edward III until a full-blown rebellious sparked in 1381. The King of 14 years old Richard II rode off to the peasants and proposing reforms, but they were not implemented. However, Richard II became a very authoritarian and impulsive ruler, with characteristics, which eventually resulted in being removed at the hand of his cousin Henry from Bolingbroke. The new king was Henry IV and becoming being the very first English monarch to use English as his main tongue in the era of the Plantagenet line, the Plantagenet line began to disengage away from their French origins, and seeing them more as Englishmen who had connections and a claim for the French throne than as Frenchmen that happened to be in England. In actual Henry IV's son Henry V, who made Chancery Standard English (Middle English) the official language for the government and that all official documents which used to be written made in Latin or French became inscribed with English.

Henry V, like Edward III claimed the French reign and continued his Hundred Years' War with France. In the Battle of Agincourt in 1415, Henry V defeated the French troops and continued to take over territories in Normandy. A few years later, in the treaty of Troyes Treaty of Troyes (1420), Henry V was named the heir to throne of France and also received the French Queen Catherine as a bride. In the midst of a dysentery epidemic, Henry VI was his son. Henry VI was crowned the King of England in 1429, and the as King of France after the demise of his father.

The fact is that this English assertion was a hotly contested particularly by the former French King's son who was the Dauphin. The Dauphin was to enjoy many military victories over English troops in France and elsewhere, it became obvious that England was unable to hold France without taking huge tolls on the country. Eventually, in 1453 in 1453, the English left for Calais. Following nearly 4100 years of territorial conflicts between William the Conqueror until Henry VI, King Henry VI, England ended in acquiring only the port of Calais and would soon also be lost. Conflict between countries and their monarchs was not averted, however the never-ending military conflicts temporarily decreased.

The Normans as well as the Plantagenets were in England as foreign rulers using French and impositioning their customs and practices upon an Anglo-Saxon state. Yet, an energizing culture exchange was taking its place, and these previously foreign sovereigns were now distinctively English as distinct from their traditional French adversaries. The English is a language that was widely spoken by people of both the common and ruling class, Geoffrey Chaucer was the leading writer of the time as well as the more exuberant architectural style brought over from mainland Europe built cathedrals and castles across England which are today considered as one of our nation's most important artifacts of culture.

Chapter 3: Thorns And Roses (1455-1603)

Conflicts in foreign lands may be lessening at present however, domestically, things reached a boil. The Plantagenets were always at odds over their control over various regions of their empire. two distinct families of the family --the Lancasters and the Yorks--did not agree on the proper occupant of the English throne. Henry VI, the current ruler Henry VI was a Lancastrian and also a flims and unreliable king. He was viewed as a threat for the nation by a lot of and especially Richard Duke of York who was a cousin of Edward III. Edward III with a claim to the English throne. In 1461, the War of the Roses, the bloody civil war was fought, and even though York was killed in battle, York was killed during the battle, his son Edward was able to continue his fight by defeating the Lancastrian troops in 1461. The king claimed the crown since Henry VI and his wife left for Scotland, Edward IV became the first Yorkist King.

The power was constantly shifting from Lancastrian as well as Yorkist forces, with Henry VI and Edward IV taking the throne in different periods, and war continued for thirty years. In the end, clever strategy from two women Elizabeth Woodville and Lady Margaret Beaufort led to the accession of younger Henry Tudor to the throne in England and ended the War of the Roses. Lady Margaret Beaufort, though a minor noble, belonged to the Lancaster family, and she saw a method to place the crown upon her son Henry Tudor. She vowed that her son would be married to Elizabeth who was York, Edward IV and Elizabeth Woodville's daughter Houses of Lancaster and York will be joined on the crown of England. When he was summoned from hiding from France, Henry Tudor landed secretly in

Wales and marched his troops towards the northeast, toward Bosworth Field. There, the controversial current Yorkist Richard III was king. Richard III met his end in 1485.

THE TUDOR ROSE

Inaugurated as the king of Henry VII of England, the king swiftly started to establish his legacy by marrying the help of his Yorkist spouse, Elizabeth. The brand new coat of arms that was adopted by the new dynasty symbolized the unification of the two houses, featuring York's white flower of York overlayed over the red roses of Lancaster which created the iconic Tudor Rose. The coat of arms was adorned all over the realm and can be seen in the beautiful chapel that he built to Westminster Abbey (Henry VII Lady Chapel). Because of the unorthodox start of his reign and his apprehension of being deposed, he was always concerned that he would be sacked, and although Henry VII was deeply shrewd and shrewd, this led him to become diplomatic and financially adept. When he died in 1509 the Treasury was bursting and he secured his children into lucrative unions. He was able to establish an agreement with Spain in the first place by the union to his son Arthur as well as later via his son's second one, Henry, to Katherine of Aragon who was the daughter of King Ferdinand and the Queen Isabella from Spain. A daughter of the King got married to the King James VI of Scotland, while the other was handed towards Louis IX of France. Louis IX of France.

The first son of Henry VII Arthur passed away before he was able to take the throne Arthur's wife and his crown passed to the charismatic and charming Henry VIII. Popular, educated and considered to be an embodiment of the Tudor Rose incarnate, Henry VIII's reign was highly anticipated all over the globe. He was initially a staunch Catholic and later labelled as a "Defender of the Faith ' according to his Pope, Henry VIII wrote his brilliant treatise Assertio Septem Sacramentorum (Defence of the seven Sacraments) as a response to Protestant attack on Papal authority made by Martin Luther.

The young and hotheaded Henry VIII had been intent to war with France in order to gain fame, just the way Henry V had on the fields of Agincourt. When his first attempts to do so failed, Henry VIII instead was advised by his advisors to stay out of conflict with France and became the most renowned peacemaker of Europe and signed the Treaty of Universal Peace with France. The Field of the Cloth of Gold in 1520 the King Henry VIII and King Francis I of France hosted a large celebration with feasting and tournaments to celebrate their newly-established relationship. Henry VIII's daughter Mary was even married to Francis I's son the Dauphin for a period of period of time.

In the British Isles, Henry VIII was also the very first English monarch to be acknowledged as King of Ireland and established control over the island by the Crown Act of 1542. The act united both nations and declared that the person who was the legitimate monarch of England will also be the legitimate ruler of Ireland.However it was bright in his first days were, dark clouds of uncertainty were soon to overtake England. Similar to his predecessors before him, Henry VIII was intent in securing his legacy as well as his dynasty by establishing the heirship of a male, as just one daughter been able to survive. Katherine the queen of his time, was tragically lost five of her children - two stillborn daughters, one unborn son as well as two sons who were not born. A desire for a male heir conjunction with Henry VIII's obsession with Lady Boleyn placed his on a collision path to the Pope of Rome and changed the way England was perceived by the world.

Looking for a method to get out of his union with Katherine from Aragon, Henry VIII claimed that because she had married by his father, God has cursed the union, preventing the couple from having living sons. The Pope was unable to allow Henry VIII an annulment, He broke away from his fellow members of the Roman Catholic Church and set himself as the Head of the Church of England. In declaring that Popish power over the nation did not serve England's interest, Henry VIII managed to utilize a burgeoning sense English pride and identity, along with a imminent threat of violence against anyone who opposed him, to fulfill his wish. The marriage he had with Katherine was annulled Their daughter Mary was branded a snob as well as Henry VIII wed Anne Boleyn and crowned her as the Queen of England.

Henry VIII's wedding to Anne did not result in an infant, though the daughter was named Elizabeth. The King would get his son Edward and his third spouse, Jane Seymour. Apart from his infamous marriage records, Henry VIII's discord from the Catholic Church would forever alter the way England had to relate to the King, since the head of the Church as well as the Head of State became one man. The Pope was for a long time the highest-ranking person in Europe However, Henry VIII sought to place himself in the same position. Henry VIII's challenge to Papal authority broke the hold of the religious terror Rome has imposed on the ruling class in Europe for centuries, and demonstrated that monarchs would no longer have their power stifled by Popes. He was an ebullient confident, proud and bold leader who made a impression on the English population and assisted in helping in establishing a strong English image on the international arena. But his most lasting contribution to the country was his beautiful red-haired daughter Elizabeth.

THE VIRGIN QUEEN

After the death of Henry VIII his three sons took the throne with speed. His son Edward VI was for the majority of his brief, young rule under the guidance of his advisors as well as powerful nobles. In the wake of his passing away, his half-sister and the daughter of Katherine of Aragon, Mary took the reigns. She was eventually referred to as Bloody Mary, she worked for years to restore England into the Catholic Church and her tactics were usually brutal and ruthless. After her death, in 1558 Elizabeth was the child of

Henry VIII and Anne Boleyn was declared the queen of England and ruled for forty-five glorious years.

Following the turbulent tussles that erupted in the conflict between Catholic as well as Protestant forces of her parents and siblings, Elizabeth I established peace between both faiths by signing the Thirty-Nine Articles in 1563; the peace likely protected her country from bloodshed and further violence that was raging across Europe during this time due to differences in religion. When England improved with Elizabeth I, the country was able to show its strength against the powerful powers that were Spain and France by sending explorers such as Sir Francis Drake out to explore new regions of the globe. Elizabeth I realized that a new era of commerce and colonization was upon the horizon and founded the East India Trading Company near the time she died in order to guarantee England's spot as one of the nations that would be a major force in the coming century.

Many other countries in Europe started to be aware of the potential for this tiny island and the dominant force of the time, Catholic Spain, testing Elizabeth I in 1588. Spain saw England as a current security threat for its faith and as a potential economic threat, dispatched an armada of large size north, with the intention to unite all of the Spanish Army out of the Netherlands in order to conquer England. While the Spanish ships crossed through the English Channel and attempted to communicate with their soldiers and the English navy launched a ferocious assault, but the attempt to invade England did not come to fruition. But, the English navy's resistance to the English is not the only reason why the Spanish Armada was unsuccessful. It was because the Spanish

Army was at risk, which made the meeting with the armada difficult The leader of the armada wasn't experienced as well, and lastly, the weather was stormy and the winds were strong, sending the Spanish ships to the north, and off the course. But, this failure by Spain resulted in a positive impact on England in the home as well as overseas. Spain had been able to take on a large empire and many English believed that the intervention of the weather as an indication that God stood with them. The commemorative medal issued at the period reads, "God blew and they were scattered."

In the reign of Elizabeth I's reign, the state definitely experienced the Golden Age of peace, prosperity and flourishing society. One of the greatest achievements to this Elizabethan Era was the work of William Shakespeare. An amazing writer, he reshaped the spheres of literature and theatre of the English literary and theatrical spheres, his works are still played, read and adapted throughout the world.

Chapter 4: A Roiling Crucible Of Revolution And Reform (1603-1801)

With the death of Elizabeth I in 1603 Henry VII and Henry VIII's greatest fears were confirmed and the Tudor dynasty did not have a direct heir. However, the closest royal cousin was located further north, in the Stuart family. Stuart family from Scotland. The King James VI of Scotland was the father of Mary who was Queen of Scots as well as Henry VII's great-great grandson. Henry VII. The king was enthralled by the south and James VI of Scotland became James I of England. The first time in history both monarchies of England and Scotland were unified under a single monarchy, however Scotland kept its individual parliaments, and also their own religious, educational and legal system. Although being the son of a strict Catholic and was raised as an Presbyterian, James I operated in a predominantly Anglican views throughout his reign. He trying to make his Church of Scotland under the similar standards of those of Church of England with the Articles of Perth in 1618.

While there were a variety of Catholic schemes to take over Elizabeth I with her Catholic cousin James I's mother and James's father, Mary, Queen of Scots the religious divides intensified throughout the Stuart family's time as a royal. The fragile tranquility Elizabeth I had achieved through her non-religious attitude was falling apart across the country. The famous and thwarted Gunpowder Plot, a Catholic plot to kill Parliament and the King James I and his son-in-law--early into the reign of King James I, caused the rise of Catholicism and a government clampdown on all remaining Catholics within the country. A separate group of individuals, Puritans were seeking to cleanse from the Church of England of any

Catholic influences, customs and rituals were growing in size and influence within Parliament.

With Catholic plots on the one hand as well as Puritan requirements to the contrary, James I rely on the divine authority to govern to maintain peace within the realm he ruled. James I had long ascribed the absolutist beliefs and written an entire essay outlining his views on the role of the monarch, The Laws of the free Monarchies. Absolute monarchies were the norm across Europe during this period as James I's contemporaries from France, Spain, and Russia each enjoying total control and power over their respective nations. The Tudors who preceded him were the Tudors were also absolutist monarchs, but they had preserved Parliament engaged, even in a nominal way. Following a series of disputes over the royal finances, a couple of years after his reign, and with James I firmly believing himself to be the supreme authority in everything, it was not surprising that the Parliament and the king seldom saw each other. James I would frequently dissolve Parliament and only call it back to session when issues with foreign or fiscal relations required the need to do so. Parliament, sitting since the year 1604, was initially dissolved by James I in 1611 then called back, as well as dissolving in 1614 and 1621 and 1624.

As there was the Thirty Years' War (1618-1648) was a war fueled predominantly by religious disagreements that raged across all continents of Europe, England found itself constantly caught in internal conflicts over religion. The son of James I, Charles I had come to the throne. Although he proclaimed the Anglican religion, he got married to with a Catholic woman, and appeared to prefer the more traditional and Catholic elements of the rituals and rites within the Church of England. Popular opinion, especially within the Parliament, was much more favour of more simple, Puritan forms of worship which had been gaining momentum after Henry VIII's split with Rome about a century before. Charles I carried on his father's practice of calling Parliament and dissolving it on an arbitrary basis, governing for 11 years in a row and never summoning Parliament to session.

In 1641, triggered by the uprising that was taking place that took place in Ireland, Charles I was required to call Parliament back to collect funds for an army. Parliament is befuddled by Charles I and unable to give him the authority to command an army, proclaimed that the army could only be led by approved Parliamentary officers. Charles I, in turn demanded every citizen who remained loyal to join his forces, and Parliament is now, in alliance along with Scottish Presbyterians, created themselves as a force in the wake of. The tensions between the Parliament and the King grew until they exploded into violent battle during the First English Civil War (1642-1646). The Parliament's New Model Army, led by Oliver Cromwell, was far more effective and disciplined than Royalist forces, and had decisive wins in Naseby (1644) in 1644 and Marston Moor (1645) coupled with Charles I's attempt to obtain military assistance against his own citizens from overseas swayed public opinion towards the Royalist campaign. Recognizing his position was not favorable, Charles I surrendered himself to the Scottish Army in the hope of being able to strike a bargain to his advantage.

Although it was a pity unfortunately for Charles I, he was transferred to English Parliamentarians through the Scottish

Army as well as placed in prison in the Isle of Wight. In the end, Charles I managed to persuade a group from Presbyterian Scots to defect to his cause, promising to back Presbyterianism in England when he returned as a king. This triggered an escalating Second English Civil War (1648) that was triumphantly won with Cromwell with his New Model Army at the Battle of Preston. Convinced by the Parliament that he was to be too risky in the event of his continued existence the king Charles I was charged with the crime of treason, and was executed in the month of January 1649. The first time in history, England was without a monarch. Parliament assumed total control of the power-swapping levers and abolished the position of the monarch in February of that year.

The decade that followed Charles I's son Charles II was reinstated as the King. Oliver Cromwell, a member of Parliament and the leader of the New Model Army, became Lord Protector of the Royal Realm. While Cromwell was king in terms of name only but the implications from this English Civil War were clear that the new ruler of England was required to be a good listener to the public and Parliament as well as cause him to lose his head. Absolutism and the divine rights of the king were in the end of their days in England.

He was crowned the King of Scotland just three years following being executed by his father. Charles II was required to leave to France after Cromwell and his troops were able to take over Scotland and declare the nation of England as well as Scotland to be one commonwealth. However, the unification could not become a fact until another 50 years, or more, until it being only achieved through the Acts of Union in 1707 under the Queen Anne. Unrest throughout Cromwell's

England along with his declining popularity policy led to that the Stuart family's, and particularly Charles II, restoration to his position two years after Cromwell's demise in 1658. Following Charles II was succeeded, the next heir to the monarchy would be James II, his Catholic sister, James II. England as a staunchly Protestant in this time and extremely wary of the newly appointed Catholic leader, and after the second wife of James II, also was a Catholic had a child, one son, concerns of a solid and stable Catholic Stuart dynasty led Protestants to look to find a better option.

The Dutch prince was the odd candidate for the throne of England however, it will not be the first nor the last time an outside power would be seated on the English the throne. William of Orange was the son of the daughter of James II Mary born from his first marriage however, most importantly both were Protestant but not Catholic. In essence, he was requested to enter England, William of Orange was able to land with his army in 1688. A large portion of the James II's troops resigned in support of William of Orange's campaign. James II stole away to France but was never to rule the throne. In the meantime, William of Orange and his wife Mary were recognized to the throne by Parliament in the role of joint rulers changing their names to William III and Mary II. Happy to have been rid of the absoluteist Stuarts The Parliament also seized this chance to get the control against the crown. They came up with an Declaration of Rights that set the royal code of conduct that limited the authority over the monarchy it dependent on the Parliament for its financial matters, and also gave Parliament the power to control the tax system and legislative process. William III and Mary II signed the declaration of the Declaration, and then they proclaimed the Glorious Revolution of 1688 established England as an constitutional monarchy.

There was not much time before another succession crisis hit England. In the event that William III and Mary II passed away without children the throne passed into Mary II's younger sibling, Anne. However, Anne even though she was having been pregnant 17 times, only managed to survive one son, who passed away at the age of eleven years old. Contrastingly, in France James II's family was still in place, and his grandson James Stuart was the closest family member and appeared to be likely to take the throne after Anne's demise. The Parliament, however, unable to allow the possibility of a Catholic succeed as king and had passed the Act of Settlement in 1701 shortly before the death of William III. The Act of Settlement not only weakened the authority of the monarchy, and affirmed the supremacy of Parliament, but also prohibited the appointment of the throne of a Catholic as a king to England. This led to Parliament was aware the succession line could be a contentious problem following the death of Queen Anne started to look for a suitable heir.

HANOVERIANS ARRIVE FROM GERMANY

Then, in Hanover, Germany, Parliament discovered the answer. Princess Sophia is a highly educated and well-read Electress of Hanover was the grand-daughter of James I and was an Protestant. In addition to having the correct blood as well as a pedigree of religious origin and a religious pedigree, it was decided that Sophia would be the next king after Anne had passed away. However, Sophia died before she was able to assume the throne as was the less well-known daughter, George, who arrived as her successor to create the Hanoverian lineage within England beginning in 1714. Many believed that he would not be worthy of the crown only one year after his reign, George I faced an revolt from the Scottish clans, who were in the support of James Stuart. While English forces ultimately won over the battle, this will not be the final armed dispute among the Scottish as well as the English about the validity of the Stuart claims.

A little English, George I was not the most popular the king. He was viewed like an outsider. He rely heavily on his ministers for his administration and frequently spent his time traveling around his property in Germany. In spite of George I's cautious approach to government and the Prime Minister's first term, Robert Walpole largely maintained power over the nation. In the meantime, Parliament had begun to break up into two parties, The Whigs along with the Tories. While the majority of Parliament was managed by Whigs, Tories were still present, and (either either in secret or openly) have backed the Stuart claims of the royal throne. Unrest and discontent against the Hanoverian King continued to be felt during George I's son George II's rule. The son of James II, Charles Stuart, "Bonnie Prince Charlie," as the father he had before was able to gather the support from the Scottish clans, and led his own Jacobite Rebellion against King George II. In 1746, during Culloden, at the Battle of Culloden, the Jacobites were crushed, and Scotland was effectively subdued. The next plot to confront the Hanoverians were very unlikely of being successful.

Yet, in spite of Hanoverian popularity, a lot of wealthy Englishmen discovered themselves following the style of their monarchs' new heirs and a particular architectural style. The style is known as Georgian, Neo-Palladian, or Neo-Classical is an rebirth of the ancient Greek and Roman designs, which is easily recognized through its colonnades, the clean and unadorned exteriors as well as cavernous, unadorned interiors. It was everywhere during the time, and even in British colonies abroad. Even to this day it is especially popular in the public and academic buildings throughout the United States, which would be a significant English colony during the time of the Hanoverian monarchs.

This awe-inspiring fascination in Greek and Roman architectural styles is also accounted for through the growth that of the British Empire began to witness. England was seen as an ideal replacement for that Roman Empire that had collapsed and retreated away from Britain several centuries before. With colonies all over the globe and an ever-growing military, and rising power in and around the British Isles, England was becoming a major power while the rival Spanish and French powerhouses began experiencing an ebb. After an embarrassing defeat to France as well as the wrath of Great Britain during the Seven Years' War (1756-1763) The colonial colonies of England as well as their influence, specifically within regions of the North American hemisphere, swelled. Although the America Colonies ended up being lost in the American Revolution (1775-1783) shortly after this momentous occasion of British supremacy, and the economy saw a little dilution because of it but the most striking fact was that England changed into an empire that was on rising. The union between Britain (England, Scotland, and Wales) and Ireland formed in 1801 and an estimated population of nine million people, England was seen as an aspiring dominating

European power that put it in a battle with the old adversaries across the Channel yet again. The English weren't the only one to believe they were the true Roman predecessors. French were able to rise from the ashes of the revolution and had chosen the first Consul General for France, Napoleon Bonaparte.

Chapter 5: The Empire's Ascendency And Apex (1801-1918)

Oacross the continent. France has become the main European power after its victory during the Thirty Years' War (1618-1648) and was able to defeat Spain and gaining European dominance for 200 years or so. France was faced with internal challenges to be certain and in 1799 an incredibly ambitious and brilliant leader known as Napoleon Bonaparte rose to power after the French Revolution. Initially, he was able to define France in the form of a republic, and declaring himself to be"the First Consul," it 5 years after his election that Bonaparte began to call himself Emperor of France as well as an official coronation ceremony was celebrated in 1804 in Notre Dame Cathedral.

Napoleon began a bloody battle, capturing a lot of Europe's vast land mass and inflicting a wrath on all of the continental powerhouses during the Napoleonic Wars (1803-1815). Great Britain, an empire growing rapidly and a major political and economic threat the expansionist ambitions of Napoleon. After three years of the Napoleonic Wars, he enacted the economic blockade against Great Britain known as the Continental System, making trade and commerce extremely difficult even though it was not the case that all European nations were willing to accept his plan. Britain's former ally, Portugal, continually resisted. In addition to causing economic hardship for England and the country, more realistic concerns started to be expressed the possibility that Napoleon might travel across the Channel and invading England the country. While there was no doubt that the British Navy was among the most powerful of all, its military could not stand an equal to Napoleon's vast and extremely well-trained Grande Armee.

While he was an clever military strategist Napoleon did make a couple of crucial mistakes that caused catastrophe for him. Some of them were the disastrous attack on Russia as well as his army's failing to conquer the Iberian Peninsula, and his loss at the Battle of Leipzig. After an European coalition was able to take over Paris because of his repeated failures and he was then forced to quit in 1814. After returning to France yet time in the 1815 war, Napoleon committed more mistakes in his Battle of Waterloo against the British and Prussian Armies. The impulsive and indecisive behavior of his as well as the dripping conditions of the battlefield enabled the British commander Arthur Wellesley, Duke of Wellington to claim victory. Devastated by the loss he suffered to his superior Duke of Wellington tactics, Napoleon was exiled to the island of St. Helena.

Following the defeat of Napoleon there was no power that could have the military or economic power to challenge Britain's power, and over the following 100 years, a Pax Britisha (British Peace) was established across the globe. In charge of a large portion of the world whether directly through colonization - there was the possibility of a British colony in almost every continent of the world at that time, or indirectly via economic manipulation, Great Britain acted as the world's policeman. It ensured peace across the globe over a period of over a century. Conflicts broke out, in the course of time however nothing of the magnitude of what Europe has faced in preceding century.

THE VICTORIAN ERA

While able to maintain only a shaky peace in the world however, in England there was an increase in tensions. In the

Industrial Revolution (1760-1840) had started a time of massive growing cities and population had risen. The cities were now crowded living and working conditions were miserable and the comparatively limited and conservative system of government in England became increasingly unsustainable with regard to contemporary pressures. In 1837, following the fact that the three sons of George III were all dead without surviving children everything was pinned on the young princess. Victoria was one of the daughters of George III's eldest son, was heir to the crown.

The Glorious Revolution of 1688 had transformed the government of the nation to become a constitutional monarchy however, it wasn't till the Victorian Era that the British Crown began to adopt its current method to operate. recognizing that the monarch was limited in power,

Victoria instead wielded her influence, not her power as a politician and was recognized, in particular during her final times, as a emblem of the British Empire. This smart shift between the monarch becoming a sovereign to a symbolic and powerful figurehead surely saved the English monarchy from the horrible fate which the majority from their European counterparts had to face between the twenties and the 20th century. under Victoria the country went through an unprecedented period of industrial expansion. Technology advancements in steamships, railroad lines and the telegraph accelerated the expanding empire because they made communication effortless. Additionally, the conservative administration's policies of laissez-faire, a hand-off method of economic policy-- allowed for huge and frequently unchecked growth. This detached style of government often resulted in disastrous consequences for people at the bottom of the social scale. There were famines. one of the most tragic examples, was the Irish Potato Famine or the Great Famine in the 1840s caused a number of deaths and an enormous flood of Irish exiles that altered the character of Ireland in general and numerous other nations that which the Irish went to.

The territory of the empire increased under the reign of Victoria and. It was regarded as the very first British monarch to become an Empress in India even though India was under the authority under the British East India Company throughout in the past century The Victorian Era firmly bound India to England in bringing it to the control of the monarch. Many times, it is referred to as"the "Crown Jewel of the British Empire," India was an extremely important part of the British Empire and added to the British economy during the duration of British rule. Today, Indian people make up one of the biggest percentages of the immigrants to the United Kingdom and have undoubtedly been a major factor in the evolution of contemporary British cultural. After the death of Victoria in the year 1901 It was said"that "the sun never sets on the British Empire."

Through the Pax Britannica, Europe had avoided the horrific violence that earlier generations had brought to the continent. But as the century of 20th century began to dawn, and when her son and grandson were taking their place in the English throne, tensions were getting underway on the continent again. Tensions were rising resulted from European the rise of nationalism, imperialism and conflicts in alliances were set to begin a conflict unlike anything previously seen in the history of mankind. Inflicting blood, violence and devastating. The Great War or World War I (1914-1918) destroyed Europe and wiped out the lives of a whole generation of youngsters.

Chapter 6: Battles, Blood, And The Death Of Imperialism (1914-Present Day)

Although the assassination attempt of Archduke Franz Ferdinand, the successor to the throne of the Austro-Hungarian Empire, in 1914 is widely believed to be the catalyst that ignited World War I, the fact is that Europe was slowly changing into a hot tinderbox over around twenty to thirty years prior to the 28th of June 1914. A string of "Mutual Defense Agreements" between diverse nations across Europe brought the entire continent of Europe into a bloody battle in a scale that was never before seen. The German Empire was a young power which was officially formed in 1871, was wary of a potential French as well as British military intervention and formed the Three Emperors' League between Germany, Austria-Hungary, and Russia in 1873. The Three Emperors' League became two following Russia was forced to leave in protest against Austria-Hungary, which was part of their Balkan States. To counter these alliances Britain began to break its long-standing "Splendid Isolation" and sought partnerships with other European powerhouses.

A frenzied look for alliances across Europe ultimately shattered the continent into two competing groups that were The Triple Alliance of Germany, Austria-Hungary, Italy as well as the Triple Entente of Great Britain, France, and Russia. There was only an act of acrimony from a single power to cause all of Europe to join the fight and roll to support their allies. Therefore the moment that Archduke Franz Ferdinand was shot in the Balkan State of Serbia, which was a long-time ally of Russia as well as the Austro-Hungarian Empire declared war against Serbia Each nation eventually took up the call from their allies and then the blazes that raged from World War I erupted.

In August 1914, Germany was invading Belgium and was marching closer towards the French frontier. It wasn't just that Great Britain allied with France by the Triple Entente however, there was an existing arrangement in place to ensure British safeguards for Belgium in The 1839 Treaty of London. Beware of the obligations they owed towards both Belgium as well as France and wary about the German Army's ability to take the entire continent of Europe under their sway, Great Britain formally entered the fight on the 4th of August 1914. It was a war unlike none other because technological advancements had surpassed methods of warfare employed by the military at the time. The same war which witnessed the first time that modern weapons like the machine guns, the heavy artillery air warfare, poison gas as well as tank warfare, were also anachronistic outfits, tonal colors and plum hats from the Napoleonic Wars complete with largely ineffective cavalry troops on horses. These old ways of warfare resulted in mass carnage as a result, and the advent of a new kind of battle was looming. The toxic chlorine gas began to fall across the battlefields and trenches were dug in Belgium and France in order to allow the soldiers the chance to wear gas masks, and provide some protection against the destruction of machine guns.

using every resource accessible in its arsenal, Great Britain had summoned troops from all over the empire. Thus, alongside a generation young Englishmen as well as a generation of younger Welsh, Scottish, Irish, Jamaican, Indian, Canadian, South African, Australian New Zealander as well as other soldiers of the Empire were wiped out. At the end of the day, Great Britain and its allies had a chance to defeat Germany as well as its allies as well as it was the Treaty of Versailles in 1919 was the catalyst that brought World War I to a conclusion. Although they were victorious but the war was a shook for Great Britain. In terms of economics, it's fair to suggest that the ravages that was World War I played a role in the dissolution of the British Empire. Morally speaking, British people were forced to look at the war while the shell-shocked youth came home and was a turning point for many of the 20th century's greatest literary talents such as C.S. Lewis, J.R.R. Tolkien, T.S. Eliot Tolkien, T.S. Eliot and others. The delight of the joy of a British victory teamed with the grave repercussions of war created large parts of modern British image, dissolving the classy and splintered society that was prevalent in the Victorian and Edwardian Eras, and paving the rise to a more democratic society. First glimpses of the new social system of welfare in England which first became apparent towards the start of the twenty-first century, gained momentum and popularity in the postwar period. In fact, the Royal Family, in the following of a virulent anti-German mood they changed their formal name from Saxe-Coburg and Gotha -- which it was prior to the reign of Queen the time of Victoria's son, King George V. the more acceptable British names of Windsor.

Following the Great War, and as the 20th century continued to accelerate, Great Britain was unable to sustain its huge empire because of a combination of nationalist and economic attitudes that were gaining traction within the colonies. It could be that the strain resulted in the collapse of other empires and to the destruction of the country that had been its home. However, in typical British style it was a matter shifting away from the imperial model in favor of one that would be more suitable in the present. From the end of the 1800s onwards, Great Britain had maintained certain control over the former colonies which had obtained some degree of independence through the classification of the colonies under the designation of "Dominions." By 1926 they Dominions were all able to swear allegiance King or Queen of Great Britain, but asserted the rights of all members in the British Empire and that The United Kingdom did not rule over the Dominions. This was the beginning of a new identity for the British Empire moving into the 20th and 21st centuries, namely The British Commonwealth. With time, many colonies became autonomous states, wishing to be part of the Commonwealth however they were not keen to swear oath to the monarchy of Great Britain. In order to rectify this issue in 1949, the Commonwealth Premier Ministers Meeting released the London Declaration which allowed republics as well as other countries outside the Commonwealth to remain or join within the Commonwealth. There are currently 54 countries that are part of the Commonwealth which is free. In allowing empires to easily merge into a commonwealth England is able to maintain an even greater presence and impact around the world than nations such as Spain and France who's empires fell apart due to the power of empires in the 19th and 20th century.

In the midst of economic turmoil all over the world during the late 1930s Germany is now to be found under Hitler began to rise in military might for the second time. In 1939, when Germany was defeated by Poland during 1939 Great Britain responded by another declaration of war. Europe was plunged headfirst into a tense global conflict only twenty-one year after the last one was over. Although the British sent troops to Europe time, the situation was quite unique and frightening for this nation. The country was historically protected from massive invasions from mainland Europe because of the English Channel The rise of air combat during the First World War had shattered the sense of safety that was cherished by the English citizens. Zeppelins were able to attack from above during World War I, but they were slow moving, heavy high-flammable, and were easily destroyed. At the time of World War II, the German Luftwaffe as well as the British Royal Air Force (RAF) were mighty fighting forces as the first air-based battle, known as known as the Battle of Britain, was battled in the skies of Europe in the year 1940. While the expertise of RAF certainly kept Nazi forces in check and prevented their plans to expand towards Great Britain, the Germans could not be stopped. An German Blitz-style bombing campaign The Blitz (1940-41) caused the destruction of huge swaths British cities and claimed many civilian lives. This led to an all-encompassing national tragedy. The ferocity experienced by civilians and soldiers during each of the World Wars forged a resilient English identity, which was well-matched with an intense nationalist sentiment that was beginning to rise throughout the 18th century. In the words of the British Prime Minister at the day, Winston Churchill said in his passionate speech in members of the House of Commons in the summer of 1940 "Let us, therefore, brace ourselves to our duties, and so bear ourselves that if the British Empire and its Commonwealth last for a thousand years, men will still say,

'This was their finest hour.'" (Churchill 1940)

The war's destruction of Europe's infrastructure as well as the massive death of people resulted in economic catastrophe. Great Britain could no longer assert itself as the dominant power of the world, in reality, America was United States, a former colony of the empire as well as geographically isolated from destruction of Europe was on the rise. In Parliament, power swung towards Churchill's Conservative Party to the more progressive Labour Party, and the modern welfare state was created, which included the establishment of the public-funded National Health Service (NHS).

In the aftermath of years of tensions After years of tension, both Ireland as well as India quit the Empire and were divided in a controversial manner to exit the doors. India was partitioned between India and

Pakistan as well as Ireland was divided into an independently Republic of Ireland and Northern Ireland and Northern Ireland, both of which were part of Northern Ireland, which remained in the United Kingdom. Problems between the United Kingdom and Ireland were recurrent for the next thirty years throughout the Troubles (1968-1998) which was an era of political tensions and violence that resulted from ethnically-based Irish organisations such as Sinn Fein, the Irish Republican Army (IRA) as well as Sinn Fein clashing with British and British-backed forces. Great Britain also joined the United Nations (UN) and the European Economic Community (EEC) that would eventually transform to become the European Union.

Through the Cold War, the United Kingdom continued to maintain strong military and economic relations to the United States and its historic allies in the

European continent. The country joined NATO. North Atlantic Treaty Organization (NATO) in the wake of increasing threats of the Soviet Bloc to the east. The year 1979 was the year that it was in 1979 that the Conservative Party came back into control with the victory of Margaret Thatcher, the first female prime minister. Similar to "Reaganism" in the United States, "Thatcherism" in the United Kingdom was characterized by its insistence on having a smaller state-run government as well as the free market which was developed through more privatization and the deregulation. While she did manage to boost efficiency in certain markets with increasing competition, and home ownership went up during her presidency however, her policies caused massive unemployment as well as recessions. According to the individual who speaks about her, she's either adored or denigrated.

In spite of influencing the affairs of throughout the world throughout the past four decades, England has remained fiercely opposed to any country or entity that would compromise its sovereign rights. The euro was first introduced in 1999 to serve as the currency to be used by the European Union, England refused and argued for the sterling pound. It could be the result that it is an island nation or maybe it's the country's past as a dominant participant on the global arena, however England is not happy with any attempt to gain authority from its European Union, and in June of this year, Great Britain narrowly voted to withdraw from its membership in EU ("Brexit"). As Brexit taking effect in the month of January 2020, there has been tensions throughout in the United Kingdom. For Scotland as well as Northern Ireland, a higher proportion of people wanted to stay in the European Union, while the majority wanted to remain in England. The rumors of Brexit could split this United Kingdom are not mere speculation. the Scottish National Party, the current largest party in Scotland is interested in calling for a new independence referendum. The outcome could be a reversal of the political union that exists between Scotland and England which has existed since 1707. In England's west, tensions is raging in Northern Ireland, similar to those of the Troubles in the last decade of the 20th century, is now on rising.

That's right. England as well as numerous other nations of the 21st century, is in a crossing point. The population demographics of the country change, and so do the requirements of its citizens. Indeed, a lot of the people who are immigrants to England are from previous colonies. And like the English have shaped their nation's history and culture and culture, they also are involved in the shaping of what is to come for the United Kingdom. Therefore, its system of government, which is both flexible and rigid throughout the decades, must be able adapt to the shifting trends of the 21st century. The future of England is impossible to predict. However, if the past is any indication that it will be just like the language it uses, constantly growing changing, always evolving, but at the same time distinctly English. George Orwell put it best, "England will still be England, an everlasting animal stretching into the future and the past, and, like all living things, having the power to change out of recognition and yet remain the same." (Orwell 1941 (p. 279).

Chapter 7: England's Prehistory - The First Inhabitants

If we talk about prehistory, the term "prehistory" typically refers to events that occurred before the advent of writing archives. In other words, prehistory is that period in time that we are not aware about. The earliest humans to have inhabited the present-day land commonly referred to as England were introduced to England around 9000 years in the past. That's why, when talking about the prehistory of England the time period runs from this point to the Roman invasion of the country at the time of AD 43.

This region has experienced important climatic, political technological, and social adjustments that scientists aren't aware about. When it comes to prehistory archeology covers three major periods, namely that of the Stone Age, the Bronze Age and the Iron Age. The designation of these particular times is derived from the technology of the time which was prevalent at the times.

Archeologists working close to Happisburgh within Norfolk discovered tools made of flint that could be traced back to around 900,000 years ago. That's incredible. People who made use of these tools are referred to as hominoids. They refer to the first humans who often traveled to England during those in the Ice Ages, when the climate was better. In the beginning, England wasn't an island It was actually an isolated peninsula that belonged to the European continent.

To give an understanding of what the terrain was from what we see now as is now known as River Thames would run into the North Sea at Happisburgh. Concerning the earliest finds by archeologists from England the remains are believed to date back 500 years ago. It is believed that they were the remains of the height of a man who stood six feet tall.

Between 9500-4000 BC the continuous occupation of England was the norm particularly because the climate was improving. In the early days, people who lived on English landscapes were hunter and gathering people. This means that they ate plant life they hunted as well as hunting wild animals.

Despite the fact that the vast majority of the peoples did not settle in the area over a long period of time however, there have been findings of settlements suggesting that there was some settlements. Also, it is believed that in the year 6500 BC because of the rise in sea levels the bridge that connected Britain to Europe was flooded, and that was the way Britain began to become an island.

Farming - A Critical Development in Human History

Experts believe that agriculture had significant impact on progress of humanity. The very first time farming was introduced into England was in the year 4000 BC. The theory is that human race that introduced different practices of agriculture to England were transported there via boat. They raised barley, pulses as well as wheat. Despite this however, they relied heavily on wild food the natural resources.

Additionally, instead of being settled within a particular area, the people relocated to different areas built on top of great public monuments. There were numerous gathering spots including the causewayed enclosure located at Windmill Hill Wiltshire, constructed in the year 3650 BC. There were several burial grounds with long barrows as well as tombs with chambers made of stone.

In the mid and late Neolithic period, various new kinds of monuments were constructed for example, timber circles such as Woodhenge or earth mounds, such as Silbury Hill. In some instances both henges and circles were interspersed. The circles of stone at Stonehenge and Avebury Both of them, dates to 2500 BC illustrate this. With regard to these kinds of monuments it's difficult to figure out the purpose and significance of their use.

As an example, Stonehenge is one of the most famous monuments of prehistoric times not just in England but across the globe. There are a variety of theories trying to understand the significance of Stonehenge, as well as the reason Stonehenge was constructed. Many archeologists and historians agree that diverse tribes contributed to the creation of the monument. This is because each section is associated with the different tribes in a sense.

Because of the variety and variety of bone, tools and various other artifacts, this idea is the most plausible. But, while we'd be interested in understanding the mystery connected with the creation of the monument, there are some things that remain a bit shady in the context of this. There is no doubt that these monuments were of great significance. certain evidence suggests that Stonehenge could have served to be a burial place. Other evidence suggests that it could be employed as a place for a ceremony. In recent times, due to the evidence of illness and injury among the human remains discovered at the location, archeologists think that the site was regarded as a site of healing. Bluestones in the past were believed to have curative powers.

With regard to these monuments, it is important to note that their design is linked to the ritual landscapes. In other words, they have a connection with other monuments built prior or later to they were constructed. For instance, in the instance of Stonehenge It was connected with Stonehenge and the River Avon.

Bronze Age in England (2300 - 800 BC)

English society has been transformed due to the development of bronze. Artifacts made of metal have been discovered in the islands, as well as in the year 2000 BC bronze was invented in England. Apart from the metal weapon and jewelry, during the same time, a different kind of pottery became popular in England known as Beaker. It's fascinating to mention that many burials were held with these items. The first metal utilized to be used in England was copper. However, later, it was replaced by bronze.

In addition, in the late and middle Bronze Age, the landscapes were marked by vast fields. Additionally individuals of that period built permanent round homes that were sometimes erected as villages. A good illustration is Grimspound located in Devon. Because of the increasing demand for land as well as security concerns hillsforts, hillforts began around the same time also.

Iron Age in England (800 BC - AD 50)

The early and middle Iron Age, people started building larger and more elaborate hillforts. Examples of this are Old Oswestry situated in Shropshire as well as Maiden Castle in Dorset. In addition, at this point the first weapons and tools made of iron. Evidence from archeology during this period suggest that, because of the high demand for military gear as well as fine metalwork at the time, it was where the aristocracy of warriors was in control.

It is believed that at this point there was a rise in tribal areas also. The first coins and the development of tribal centers go back to the end of the Iron Age. In addition, it was at this period that people first made contacts directly with Roman world. This time also is also the time when we first record documents of life on the island. The most well-known records are of Julius Caesar - as he was a rogue in the years 55 and 54 BC.

In the accounts of this period the religious leaders referred to as Druids were also included along with chariot wars. After Caesar's raids Romans took over the region with the primary difference being the fact that they hoped to remain.

Chapter 8: The Roman Invasion And Its Legacy

The earliest written documents of English historical events date to the time of the Roman Conquest in 43 AD. In the past, Julius Caesar was the first Roman ruler to conquer his goal of the British Isles, but it was the Emperor Claudius that essentially finished his mission in a sense. This is because he commanded an invasion of the region. Within a brief period of time, the Romans were able to control the tribes in the southeastern region of England. The chieftain was a particular one from the Catuvellauni tribe, known as Caractacus, who fled off in South Wales. He fought against the Romans until he was killed and then captured by the Romans in the year 51 AD.

The main factor that ensured the victory that led to the success of Claudian invasion was that a total of 40000 soldiers from the military arrived in England under the direction of Aulus Plautius. Regarding the Romanization process, which was the introduction of unique Roman traits in the lives of indigenous peoples, it took place predominantly in the lowerlands zone more specifically, south and east of Lincoln up to Exeter. The Romans created a new area of the Empire. It was called Britannia.

The previous Iron Age tribal centers were transformed into Roman towns that had all of the usual Roman features - including streets with regular grids, basilicas, the market squares, bathhouses and temples as well as the theaters, the shops centres, amphitheaters, hostels as well as other.

The models and design of the buildings were Roman however, the towns were built by the local gentry as a significant portion of residents embraced Roman methods of living. In other words, the wealthy class of England took on a new way of living. This is the reason why there wasn't massive number of foreign rulers living in England The local population who were in return for their property and power were able to accept their rights to the Romanization process.

In What Ways Did the Romans Change England?

In the beginning, there was no country at all, therefore, it is impossible to ignore how significant an impact Romans were able to have on the progress of England. In this regard, as there was a time when the Roman Empire was in difficulty as Rome was attacked, the capital city Rome was struck by a guerrilla, Britain was left on its on its own. In other words, they had to deal the whole thing all on their own. This was initially quite difficult. After that, there was chaos as indigenous tribes and foreign invaders battled for dominance. This is why a lot of individuals decided to return to their rural homes This is the reason that many of the cities founded by the Romans were destroyed.

However, despite the chaos immediately the following day, there were other consequences that were much more important. In essence, when the Romans first landed into what would eventually become English area, they incorporated their own style of life by introducing a process known as Romanization. One of the modifications made to the area by Romans was the system of roads. Prior to the advent of the Romans it was dirt tracks. Thus, what the Romans constructed was more than 10,000 miles of brand new roads throughout the country.

In order to ease the process of transport, they created roads as effective as they could. Roads were constructed from an underlying of clay as well as gravel and chalk. Then, on top of that they Romans laid large smooth stones. So that rainwater was able to run off, the layout of roads had ditches. It is important to note that certain roads constructed by the Romans remain in use in the present day, particularly the major roads. Other routes were converted into motorways.

There are Roman remains that remain present to this present. The most notable sites is Hadrian's wall. The wall was built to define the boundaries between the Roman Empire and to highlight the difference of Roman Britain as well as Scotland in the period of moment. It was long at 73.2 miles, and stretched between Wallsend-on-Tyne up to Bowness.

Another significant mark left behind by the Romans is the practice of bathing that was made possible by the construction of public baths. It is the reason why should you decide to go to Bath it is possible to be amazed at the qualities of the city as it brings one to Rome. Bath situated in Somerset was a city in which people went to relax cleanse, stay clean, be healthy and make people they knew. The main reason the Romans decided to choose Bath was the fact that the bath is naturally heated because there are rocks beneath the earth.

It is also important to consider the effect the Romans made on religious beliefs. Naturally they were Britons were pagans. This means that they worshipped a variety of gods to worship. In the case of the Romans who were also pagans, they are also, except that they worshipped various gods. However, they didn't prevent the Britons from praising their gods of their own, provided they respected Roman gods, too. The only difference was that it wasn't until the second century when Christianity was introduced to English territory. It was at first that Christianity was not accepted by Romans because the adherents of this religion were being slandered. Constantine was the very first Roman Emperor to allow the people to adhere to Christianity In AD313, Constantine declared that Christians could worship God with peace.

Concerning the manner in which towns were organised, it might be interesting to note that the Romans in the end changed their way of life. They embraced the concept of living in large cities and towns. At the time of the Roman Empire, towns were laid out in grids with the center of the city having a forum or large market, where traders would meet to exchange trade. Did you realize that London was one of the Roman city as well? It was initially called Londinium. It was named Londinium when the Romans built a fort on the River Thames, as this was the place where traders came from across the empire to sell their goods into Britain. The city grew until it was the largest and most powerful city in Roman Britain.

Chapter 9: The Anglo-Saxon Period - The Birth Of England

If you're interested in English culture The colonization program that was initiated by the Anglo-Saxons merits noting. When we talk about Anglo-Saxon England it refers to a period in English historical times when Roman influence gradually diminished in favor of the creation in the Anglo-Saxon kingdoms. It was in the 5th century. the Anglo-Saxon time period continued until 1066. Norman Conquest of England in 1066. Historical scholars refer to the 5th and 6th centuries in the development of England as the Dark Ages, archaeologically being called Sub-Roman Britain.

After that, the kingdoms of Anglo-Saxon began to be created. It's a challenge to determine a unified chronological chronology in relation to the dispersal of Romans from Britannia. While this is reported through Geoffrey of Monmouth in Historia Regum Britanniae however, some historians have questioned whether the data presented in the text is based on Medieval stories or it is not. As evidenced by archeological excavations from the last period in Roman rule, scholars are able to establish the presence of clear signs of decline. The coinage was not minted as frequently in the years after 402. In the meantime, with regards to the introduction of the Anglo-Saxons to Britain, there are a variety of myths and legends. Some originate from historical facts, while others don't.

The Anglo-Saxons: From Where Originated They? And Which Place Did They Reside in England?

The Anglo-Saxons are essentially people who migrated from the northern part of Europe as part of the Germanic population. They were initially organized into small groups, which would create a variety of kingdoms. The Anglo-Saxons eventually could unite within a certain geographical area, namely the Kingdom of England. It happened under the time of the King AEthelstan. Prior to the arrival of the Normans during the 11th century, Anglo-Saxons were the main power in England.

According to sources, the Anglo-Saxons initially resided in the eastern part of England. Then, they turned their focus westwards and northwards in order to establish the area in which Britons were to live. Gildas and Bede are writing from the point of view that of an Briton as well as the perspective of a Northumbrian. Thus, they present the story of the struggle between Britons and Anglo-Saxons declaring that their coming was punishment by God. In other words, the Britons were forced to pay for their leaders were depraved.

Additionally, they didn't refer to themselves as such. It is believed that this name was coined around the 8th century as a way to distinguish the Germanic-speaking population that lived in England. In addition, it is important to note that they also spoke the same language that we refer to as Old English. This means that the modern language of English has its roots in the Anglo-Saxon language.

Because of the existence of manuscripts in Anglo-Saxon England Specialists have identified that, in every part of the country there was a distinct dialect spoken. For instance, Northumbrian, West Saxon or Mercian. The most ancient English poem, namely the Caedmon's Hymn composed using Northumbrian. Northumbrian dialect. English. Following the Viking Invasion of England, which took place in the 9th century Old Norse was also widespread in both eastern and northern England.

The Religious Beliefs of the Anglo-Saxons and Christianization (600-800)

In analyzing the characteristics of culture of a group the religion of a group is something to take into consideration. In this regard, the Anglo-Saxons who first settled in England were pagans and historians wouldn't have had much information about their religion If they hadn't found evidence concerning their burial practices. So, upon the conclusion of burials in cemeteries that date back to the Anglo-Saxon period, historians have been able to demonstrate that the Anglo-Saxons utilized cremation in lieu of inhumation. Furthermore they were also known for their tradition of burial for the most valuable possessions they owned with their remains, which suggests they believed in the afterlife. In the same way,

Bede has pointed out that the names given to each month of the year are rooted in the pagan symbolism of each month.

In the midst of 600 CE, however in the year 600 CE, the gradual Christianization that was taking place in Anglo-Saxon England began. In essence, this was because of the Roman Catholic Church and the expansion of Celtic Christianity from the northwest. Pope Gregory the Great sent the Italian monk Augustine to England to make King AEthelberht of Kent. In 601, Augustine received the baptism of the first Anglo-Saxon King to Christianity. By 800 CE it was believed that the Christianization of the Frankish Empire was almost completed.

In the 7th and 8th century, the authority of England was divided between the larger and more powerful Anglo-Saxon kingdoms. According to the records of

Bede, Aethelbert of Kent was the most powerful one during the sixth century. After that, power was passed to the Kingdom of Northumbria to the north.

But the dominance of Northumbria ended through two battles, The Battle of Trent (679) against Mercia as well as the fight against the Picts in Nechtansmere (685). The 8th century was the time, it was the time of an alleged Mercian Supremacy. While it was not constant both of the most powerful monarchs, namely Aethelbald and Offa retained their authority as well as their status. Offa's Dyke can be seen as an example that demonstrates the mighty power of Offa his ability to build something of this magnitude. The ability to gather all the required resources to create the structure of this magnitude is remarkable for the era.

However, as a result of rising competitiveness of the smaller kingdoms, aswell in the increasing strength of Wessex The Mercian Supremacy ended up coming to an ending.

The 9th Century: The Coming of the Viking and the Rise of Wessex

The initial officially sanctioned Viking attack was recorded in 793, near Lindisfarne monastery, as per the Anglo-Saxon Chronicle.

The Anglo-Saxon Chronicle contains a set of journals that are written using Old English, and they tell the story of the Anglo-Saxons. They are believed to have were written by Wessex probably under the reign of Alfred the Great which is a significant historical figure for English historical records.

However, as there are a small number of remaining fragments that are part of an Anglo-Saxon Chronicle, it is probable that additional Viking raids took place prior to the date. It's worthwhile to point out that Anglo-Saxons were an extremely educated society, which means that a large portion of their population could to write and read. Before 1100, more than 1000 books were published and possessed in England and included books, prayers, Bibles and saints' lives and biographies, monastic documents as well as so and so on.

The King Alfred of Wessex was a key contributor to improving literacy in England and this is the reason why he fought for the translation of crucial works of Latin into Old English. The King Alfred of Wessex is a key character in English the history of England We'll discuss details about his role in a future part.

Going back to the Viking invasion, following an array of Viking attacks in the early years, Vikings began to settle in England. Because of the presence the existence of Danish as well as Norwegian settlements in the area, the English spoken language was significantly affected and many phrases used in the modern English are derived in Old Norse. But, the vast majority of the words that are commonly used in contemporary English come of Old English. Additionally, during the ninth century one the biggest events of that time would be the emergence of the kingdom of Wessex.

Alfred the Great - King of Wessex

Alfred is a prominent name within English historical records, not just due to his resistance to the Viking attack, but also due to the fact that Alfred was the prime initiator of a number of important social reforms. That's what makes him the only English monarch who is known as"the Great. From 871 to 899 AD the king was in control over the Anglo-Saxon kingdom building a strong military and was a powerful administrator and advocate for reforms. Thanks to his leadership that the invasion by the Danes was thwarted, setting the groundwork for an Anglo-Saxon society that was united.

Following the victory of Alfred, Alfred triumphed over the Danes and the Danes, a treaty was made, under which the Danes had control over the east and north while Alfred as well as the Anglo-Saxons will be in the control over Kent, West Marcia and the Kingdom of Wessex. The king was convinced it was the necessity to protect the kingdom. That's why he wanted to transform and improve the existing Army structures and implement new strategies and methods.

Also, he wanted to create the navy strong enough to keep pace with the Danes with their supremacy in this field. To ensure that there was enough money to finance the various reforms and programmes the tax and conscription program was put in place. The amount was determined based upon the efficiency of the landowner's tenant. This was a crucial aspect in the safety of the coming kingdom.

Furthermore, Alfred revolutionized the way that society was organized and structured. Alfred desired that judges demonstrate a variety of important characteristics, including being well-read, knowledgeable, possessing a profound knowledge of law, and an excellent educational background.

But, the most significant step was bringing together the kingdoms which had existed separately up until that point. One could say that under the guidance by Alfred the Great that the Anglo-Saxon society was successfully shaped and refined. In the above paragraph, Alfred appointed to write the Anglo-Saxon Chronicle, a document that emphasized the importance in the unified England. In addition it also reveals it also provides insight into the history of England. Anglo-Saxon Chronicle also supplies insight into the characteristics of English society of the time.

Also, he reformed the education system by highlighting the significance in Old English, making books and education widely available to those interested in intellectual pursuits. In addition, he set up courts to provide an education that was good not just to the people of the nobility, but as well for those who did not have a status of social standing. The legacy he left is an amazing legacy because he was able to reform and change the structures of Early English society, ensuring peace despite the uncertainties and creating the security and stability. The impact of his work was significant to the generations following.

The Legacy of the Anglo-Saxon Period

Some historians believe it was in the period known as the Anglo-Saxon era when England flourished as it were. The many features which would later define England through the years can be traced in this time, such as the evolution of the Language - specifically, in particular, the fact it was Old English would come to replace Latin and was employed throughout Europe.

Additionally It was also Alfred, the King Alfred who initiated programmes to stop to the plight of children who were illiterate and increase literacy. In addition It was because of Alfred's victory over and against the Vikings which England was able to be saved. That's also the reason that was the reason he became King of Anglo-Saxons. Alfred was also influenced to become a king by his experience with the Carolingian Renaissance, according to that all Christian monarchs must be in the first place, advocates of knowledge.

A further significant legacy left by Anglo-Saxons is their contribution to establishing the basis of English the legal system. In other words, in 928 the first legal code that would be applicable to everyone in England was drafted in the reign of King AEthelstan. This is primarily the reason that many historians claim that this was that year it was that the English state was established and paved the foundation to the English Parliament, which was a success in many ways.

There's an important English law book dating through the period of time, in particular, the Codex. It contains the first works that were written in English that include codes and laws that document the conferences of Alfred's grandson, AEthelstan, when he met with members of the council on questions of laws, punishment as well as crime. In addition, they were preaching in the language spoken by their own nation, which was not commonplace. The earliest English gospels are traced to the time of the Anglo-Saxons.

Chapter 10: The Norman Invasion - What It Meant For England

A significant incident that is significant in English historical records is The Norman invasion. Who was those Norman people? The Normans were pirates of the pagan barbarian religion that came from Denmark, Iceland, and Norway They conducted a number of attacks against European settlements along the coast. The invasion began around the eighth century. In the 9th century that rate of their attacks increased in the west coast of France. They eventually absorbed the traits of early medieval European society, embracing the chivalry rules, abstaining from paganism, and adhering to traditional Christian standards.

In this context the pivotal moment of English historical events can be traced to 1066 which was that year in which came the Norman Conquest. The year 1066 was when William the Conqueror (Duke of Normandy) came to England to take the throne. Before this however, the Saxon King, Harold II, had defeated the Norwegian Viking Army led by Harald Hardrada. Harald Hardrada, thus putting an ending to the Viking period.

William's triumph in The Battle of Hastings - which led to the death of Saxon King Harold II - secured the complete control over England through the Normans. It was an important incident in English historical events - and partly changing the way England was largely far away from Continental Europe till that point. An additional important factor is the historical fact that William was the one who commissioned the creation of the Domesday Book.

Domesday Book or the Book of Winchester and Its Importance

What was the Domesday Book? This was an important survey of England that was published in the year 1086 CE. For a better understanding of what this meant we must understand that this survey is similar to what we call an agreement today, which was initiated by the state. What was the goal of this study and why was it important? It was essentially, William commissioned it in an effort to find out what percentage of the land was held in England and who owned it. It was also important to determine the amount they would be taxed based on the property they held.

Furthermore the book also provides an extensive overview of the ways in which early medieval society was run. If the Domesday Book had not been created, it could be extremely difficult to present the English society during the 12th and 11th the 12th century. We could say that the

Domesday Book showcases the Norman ability to organizing and establishing order.

Social Hierarchy within The Social Hierarchy in the Anglo-Norman Society When it comes to Norman rule of England there are numerous references to the known as the Norman Yoke. The term was used extensively by revisionists who emphasized the oppression and tyranny which was placed on those who were under it during the time that the Normans came into Anglo-Saxon England. To put it in perspective one of the major changes made by William was his implementation of feudalism. To secure the power of his family, William brought noblemen and provided them with castles and land all over the country as a reward for their loyalty. This was not a popular choice by a large section of the population, in sens that the Saxon gold age was obscured through the granting of nobility as well as gentlemen to rule over the English the land.

It was the key strategy that enabled William to gain dominance and English the throne as William was not regarded as the king of England from the beginning. A feudal system led to the kingdom was then split into distinct areas of land, which were just as large as the counties that we have in the present. These land parcels were also administered by noblemen who fought alongside William during the Battle of Hastings.

The nobles must swear to their loyalty and were accountable for tax collection in their respective regions, as well as offering the king troops in the event of a request. This is the main reason William the conqueror was regarded as a brutal leader. But, since William conquered England and conquered the country with force, he needed to ensure his authority through the use of the system of feudalism was considered to be the best way to do this. In addition the changes led to the establishment of a central governance.

Other Changes Brought by the Normans

With regard to the impact from the Norman Conquest, the landscape of the nation was altered by the fact that castles were constructed all over the countryside. The castles that were built in the country are a hallmark of Norman rule, and were given to nobles. It was the start of a new era in the construction of amazing, stunning stone structures that could stand up to many centuries. Also, they modernized the building of cathedrals and churches.

The arrival of the Normans was also influential in the growth of the English language and its culture. In during the

Anglo-Saxon time period, the only language most frequently used in the English language was Old English. But during the Norman rule was a return to Latin.

Furthermore according to historians and historians, the Norman aristocracy was the basis for the strongest monarchies across Europe and the impact it had on the evolution of a sophisticated government system. The conquest had a profound effect on English cultural practices, and may have set the stage for the widely-popular conflict among England and France and France, which would continue into the twentieth century.

Chapter 11: The Middle Ages In England

Historical scholars argue it was historians believe the Middle Ages in England lasted up to 1066, until 1487, when Wars of Roses ended in 1487. The period was a time when England faced both international and civil war and political intrigues within the royal elite, rebellion and more. In this section in which we'll concentrate on a few of the most important elements and events of English historical events.

Magna Carta

With no fear of contradiction the signing and enactment of Magna Carta in 1215 had profound effects that shaped England in the way we see it in the present. Magna Carta is Latin for the Great Charter or the Great Paper and is known as Magna Carta Libertatum or the Great Charter of Freedoms. It was basically the basis for what would later eventually become the law of the Constitution that we have in the present.

Magna Carta had a profound impact on countless legal documents of the common law and documents, not just in English historical context, but also the United States Constitution, as and the Bill of Rights, for example. The historians have indicated that the Magna Carta represents one of the most significant and influential documents that have ever existed in the history of the American democracy.

It was essentially created in response to numerous disputes among the pope Innocent III, King John, and English barons in the course of how they debated the rights of King. In the Magna Carta, the king must surrender some rights as well as comply with a number of legal processes, which indicated that the wishes of the monarch was bound to the laws.

There are many misperceptions concerning the development of Magna Carta, you should be aware that it contained a variety of basic principles related to rights of the human person, which was the foundation for a democracy. Through the years it was a fact that Magna Carta was modified and revised. Even to this moment, it is one of the major influences in the long-running historical development that established constitutional law.

The English Reformation

When we talk about the English reformation, most of us focus on the part of Henry VIII - who purposefully separated from and reformed the Roman Catholic Church. The seeds for reform were already planted by a hundred years earlier. Before the Reformation, strength and authority of Pope Francis were unquestioned and were considered to be absolute, so to say. John

Wycliffe played an important role in the reformation of the English church, since the time he is an English theologian, who devoted his time to provide the first English version from the Bible.

His beliefs were often in contrast to the doctrines espoused in the works of Calvin and Luther as well as other significant European reformers. That's why his name was coined as the Morning Star of the Reformation. But he would also be condemned by an Papal Bull at the beginning of the 15th century. Henry VIII was King Henry VIII would be the person who would initiate to the English Reformation, essentially making an end of his Roman Catholic Church and establishing his own position as the Head of the Anglican Church.

The Tudors and How They Influenced England

The Wars of Roses basically came to an end with the war was won through Henry Tudor - or Henry VII. It marked the start of the Tudor period that lasted until 1603 when of Elizabeth the Queen Elizabeth came to an end.

One of the most well-known English reigning monarchs Henry VIII is mostly famous for the fact that he was the first monarch to break off from the Roman Catholic Church, which caused the formation of the separate Church of England. Furthermore it was also his intention to pursue the dissolution of monasteries and he also unified England as well as Wales. It also resulted in the establishment of Henry as the leader of the Church, with his contribution to the church being mostly linked to the birth of the English Reformation.

While he initiated the Reformation because of political motives, rather than religious reasons but it happened, and ultimately, it changed the appearance of England. Henry's private life wasn't ideal however, once his claim to the throne of the Church in the early 16th century, he gave England an entirely new position in the world and thus shifting its status.

Instead of trying to get the approval of Rome, England now focused on its own country by focusing on the things that made it special, and this will eventually lead to the expansion of imperial power that was to take place in the next century. According to the historians, it was an important moment in the development of England. With the expansion of imperial power it was evident that the principles in the foundations of democracy - specifically, political and religious liberties continue to be in use in both the United States and the Commonwealth.

That's why, when considering Henry VIII's lasting legacy it is possible to think about how England was viewed following his death, not a part of Europe in general and directed towards all of the globe. However, that doesn't mean England did not participate in any European issues, especially considering that, in the ensuing centuries it would be fighting the Spanish Armada and the Spanish Armada in the Napoleonic Wars as well as during the Two World Wars. In parallel with this, England's Church of England would develop to become a powerful Protestant church that sent missionsaries across what would eventually turn into what would become the British Empire and not only.

Henry VIII was survived by three children, one of them legitimate and two illegal. The sole legitimate heir to the crown was Edward VI of England, who took the throne in his 10th year of age and then died because of tuberculosis. Mary I succeeded to the English throne and, since she was a devoted follower of Catholicism and tried to make it a law. However she resented Protestants and burned no less than 274 Protestants. Her reputation was not well-liked by her people. Elizabeth I succeeded her, yet another English monarch, who was regarded as being one of the most powerful monarchs, not just in English history, but also in the historical history of Europe too.

Her reign brought about a certain amount of calm in the country that was largely chaotic. To deal with the conflict between religions that had been in the air over England from the 16th century onwards and to establish an institution called the Elizabethan religious Settlement. It played an important role in the development of the Church of England. In addition, it is important to note that the settlement was a reassessment of the separation of the English church from Rome by granting the Parliament of Elizabeth with the status of the Supreme governor of the Church of England. Through an Act of Uniformity in 1559, it established what form of the English Church was bound to accept, as a result of the creation to the Book of Common Prayer, in addition to other items.

The reality that England was to become an economic force of prominence in the years that followed could also be traced back to Elizabeth. In essence, she gave John Hawkins the right and authorization to begin trading in commerce in 1592. Furthermore she also introduced slavery to England. In a way, it was through the trade in slaves that England became an empire. Actually the amount of slave Africans was so huge that Elizabeth was not happy with the situation. Thus, with the help of an Proclamation in 1601 she tried unsuccessfully to remove them.

Under the reign of Elizabeth, England accomplished great battles in the field. In contrast historical critics had a hard time with her for the reason that she was a supporter of the English slave trade, in addition to the tense circumstances within Ireland in the period of her rule. In the meantime, Elizabeth directed England towards an imperialism, which meant that the country pursued an overseas position, thus making it a part of Europe. However, Elizabeth demonstrated that women are also capable of being efficient and strong monarchs.

Chapter 12: The 17th And 18th Centuries In England

Through the creation plants in Ireland that began in 1608 England established a model for the establishment of colonies. A few of those who were involved in these projects also contributed to the beginning of colonization in North America - such as Walter Raleigh, Humphrey Gilbert and Ralph Lane, among others.

In the process, around the start of the 17th century England built a new establishment within Virginia (Jamestown) in the 17th century, which would later be renamed The United States of America, which would mark the beginning of English colonization of America. With the abundance of opportunities offered by the colonies, lots of English individuals decided to establish themselves on the continent of North America, as it was extremely lucrative due to the abundance of opportunities. This is the reason why in the second half of 17th century witnessed an increase in the amount of people leaving for North America. New World.

A lot of people chose to move in North America in order to enjoy religious freedom. Then, shortly afterward, English merchants who ran the plantations of the south of America adopted slavery as a way of increasing their income while reducing their expenditure. Native Americans and imported Africans were employed for this.

It was through the English colonization of the country that the landscape of England ended up changing, literally. Thanks to their rapid accumulation of riches The fortunes of English merchants were increasing every day. As they had more cash to spend, it led to the development of a middle class of England and changed the political balance. In the beginning, the most prosperous and significant colonies for the economic health of the country were situated in the Caribbean that produced sugar. In the Caribbean, slavery played an important role.

The English Civil War

We'll now look at another significant event in the historical development of England which is the English Civil War, or the English Civil Wars. The wars refer to various conflicting armies between Parliamentarians as well as Royalists between 1642 and 1651. Also, these conflicts occurred between those who believe that the monarchy should be given all-powerful and undisputed authority as well as the supporters of Parliament that should ensure that the authority of the monarch under control.

In the year Charles I succeeded the English throne in the year 1815, England was experiencing a time of peace. Charles wanted to join the three kingdoms that were England, Scotland, and Ireland into a single kingdom by fulfilling his father's wish (James I. of England). This was not favored by many parliamentarians as they were concerned that the establishment of the kingdom would mean that the end of English customs that had founded the monarchy. However, Charles' viewpoint of the monarchy was that the monarch ought to have complete power and be in a position to exercise this power.

The eruption of conflict seemed likely. The war ended with Battle of Worcester on the 3rd September 1651 which was the day of victory for the Parliamentarians. This resulted in it was the English monarchy was replaced by the Commonwealth of England (1649 - 1653) as well as later to become an Protectorate (1653 to 1655) which was then governed by Oliver Cromwell. But in 1660 Charles II was restored, becoming the successor to the monarchy. From a constitutional point standpoint, because of the conflicts, there was a precedent set in England. In this regard the monarchs were not able to rule the nation without the approval of the Parliament. But, this idea could have been essentially sealed following the Glorious Revolution.

The Glorious Revolution

In the wake of the death of Charles II in 1685 the Catholic brother was the next to be named the King James II & VII. However, given the history to the English Reformation, having a Catholic King was unimaginable for the majority of people. This was what eventually caused the Glorious Revolution that resulted in the removal of James II of England from the throne, and then bringing William from Orange to take his place.

It is vital to evaluate how important The Glorious Revolution in shaping the ideas that form the basis of the English monarchy. The reality that James was thrown out of the crown exemplified the values of democratic democracy in the present that are in place until this very moment. In other words, the monarch does not enjoy the power of all-powerful authority. In the same way, it established the Bill of Rights as being an important document in national history of politics. As it was the time that Roman Catholic James II was put aside, it ended any chance of Catholicism getting reestablished in England.

In the end, the Glorious Revolution is one of the major developments in the history of the role that the crown played and the parliament of England. When as the Bill of Rights was passed and the Bill of Rights was enacted, the chance for the monarch who held Catholic convictions to take over in the English throne was eliminated. The Bill of Rights, however the Bill of Rights crayoned the limits of authority and power of the monarch in running a nation.

In this way, it is possible to say that the Bill was a crucial element for the not-written British Constitution, since it conferred the supreme authority on Parliament, by restricting the authority of the monarch. Therefore, the king could no longer be able to tax as well as suspend laws or have an army that was in place during periods of peace, without the consent of Parliament. It is believed that the Bill of Rights also influenced the U.S. Bill of Rights.

From 1689 onwards, England - - which was to in the future become known as The United Kingdom - has had the statutory as an constitutional monarchy. From then on the power of Parliament was increased, while that of the crown waned.

The Foundation of the United Kingdom

The period of the 18th century was the beginning of the United Kingdom. As per the Acts of Unification 1707, England and Scotland - who had been united prior to 1707 - the Union of the Crowns in the 17th century, agreed to create an political union. This was the beginning of the united kingdom of Great Britain. It was the Acts of Union represented a collection of Parliamentary Acts that were passed by the Parliament of England as well as Scotland. In essence, following many years of conflict an unification on a voluntary basis was achieved for the mutual benefit of both countries.

In this regard From 1707 onwards, England was no longer an individual political entity. It still has influence in the United Kingdom of Great Britain as well as Northern Ireland. The major influence on the economy and politics within the United Kingdom was still derived from England, London developing as the capital of the country.

Chapter 13: The 19th And 20th Centuries In The History Of England - Key Events That Left A Mark

After the defeat of Napoleon Bonaparte in the Napoleonic Wars (1804 - 1815), England soon became the world's most powerful navy power of the early 19th century. The British Empire, at its highest point, was the biggest empire ever built, maintaining its standing as a key worldwide power for an extended period of. The 19th century was also an era of change for England as a result of the Industrial Revolution, as it was a key player of the revolution so to speak.

The Industrial Revolution

At first, England had a leading role during the Industrial Revolution that initially started at the close of the 18th century. It was however during the 19th century that the most technological advancements took place, which would influence the mechanical process, which transformed the agrarian system.

If we had to define the Industrial revolution, we'd need to mention that it revolutionized the way the way people lived and performed their jobs. Changes were made throughout a wide range of industries which included medicine, technology education, economy as well as culture and society. These new technologies replaced humans' labor for mechanical. Thus, the start of the Industrial Revolution marked a critical event in the human story but not only within the historical background of England. Though it's rooted in England however, it had an impact on every part of the globe.

In the Industrial Revolution, many people began to migrate from countryside towards cities. In contrast as a result of the development of factories that were large, many small towns were transformed into cities throughout the years. The rapid growth of cities in England caused a number of problems as the towns were crowded and struggling with unsanitary sanitation, pollution as well as the absence of drinking water.

In addition, despite the reality that industrialization improved the standard of living for people of the upper and middle class, those in the lower classes had to struggle with financial issues. It was a tedious job and sometimes dangerous, since they had to operate all kinds of machinery, not to not mention the hours of work that were long and strenuous. Pay was also not high. The reality is that the opposition was strong against industrialization, that was initiated by Luddites who were well-known for their violent resistance against the introduction of reforms to the manufacturing industry in England.

In a completely different way in the early part in the late 19th century workers were struggling to define and find their voice. Industry's concentration led to the formation of guilds and unions that eventually became powerful enough to resist government policies. The history of the world believes that the beginnings of Chartism could date back to 1832, when it was the time that the Reform Bill was passed. According to the Reform Bill, the greater majority of men in middle class was given the right to vote apart from those in the middle class.

Victorian England

The Queen Victoria was the longest-lasting English monarch. She ruled Britain for over 60 years. Through this time it was a time when the nation grew in prosperity and strength. Her reign was the culmination of the Industrial Revolution in England, and also the power over Britain. British Empire.

In the Victorian Age, Britain was the most powerful nation and the Victorians believed that to ensure the stability of the country the country needed to maintain peace. The Queen Victoria was a major advocate during the Industrial Revolution, promoting the creation of an advanced railway system, which would allow transport over the following decades.

World War I (1914 - 1918)

The First World War was a world-wide conflict that altered the development of Europe during the early 20th century. The war was fought among both the Entente Powers - represented by France, Russia, the United Kingdom, eventually joined by Italy as well as the US in the United States - as well as the Central Powers represented by the Austro-Hungarian, German and Ottoman Empires. In the aftermath of the revolutionary movement in Russia The country retreated from the war in.

The time of war was when there was an overwhelmingly sentiment of anti-Germany among people which is why it was decided that the Royal Family decided to relinquish any titles that were part of the German crown. They also substituted names that sounded German for ones which resembled the English the language better.

In the aftermath of the chaos and devastating consequences during the Great War, Britain remained an significant power. The Empire reached its peak following the granting of its League of Nations mandate over colonies that were previously controlled under The German as well as the Ottoman Empires. In 1921, the extent of the British Empire was quite astonishing and included more than 458 million approximately one-quarter of the inhabitants of the world.

The English tradition would grow more prevalent - particularly within public domains, such as the governmental and legal structures, for example, in the practice of economics and military as well as the manner that the education system was conducted, in sports as well as the increasing acceptance of the English the language as well as Anglican Christianity.

In 1922, it was the year that Independence for the Irish Free State caused the splitting of Ireland. In 1927, it changed the name of the nation in its current name to United Kingdom of Great Britain as well as Northern Ireland.

World War II (1939 - 1945) World War II (1939 - 1945) Second World War was another important conflict that had a profound influence, and it basically combined two conflict - one within Asia called the Second Sino-Japanese War, and the second one that took place in Europe by the incursion of Poland. The world's nations were split into two groups - The Allies in addition to the Axis.

England was engaged in the war on with its Commonwealth allies, which included Australia, Canada, South Africa, New Zealand, and India and was later joined by allies from other countries. As the war was a global one and resulted in the deaths of over 60 million people. This could be the most fatal ever, and the most catastrophic incident that mankind has ever experienced. The conclusion of the war was marked by the triumph of the Allied group - England as a member of the Allies.

Winston Churchill - a critical personage during Winston Churchill - a key figure in the World War - and his successor Clement Atlee contributed to creating an effective postwar society. Despite this following the war, England was struggling financially as well as physically. Because of the difficulties in the current situation, it needed to obtain loans in both the United States and Canada - the loans were extremely costly.

In the end, due to Marshall Aid, England steadily recovered during the latter half in the second decade of 20th century. Marshall Plan Marshall Plan was a plan established in the United States, according to that it was to aid the nations that were allied with Europe following the devastating outcome that was World War II. This was to create an economic stability and a democratic government within Western Europe, while facilitating the establishment of a security alliance known as NATO. However there was a time when the US became a world power and this could be said of that of the Soviet Union. The US was the first to establish an era of Cold War that would define the subsequent 45 years.

In the aftermath of World War II, most of the countries that were part to the British Empire before the war were made independent. There were also other states who decided to join to the Commonwealth of Nations, which was a non-profit association of states that were independent.

Chapter 14: England Travel - Tips For A Worthwhile Experience

England is a beautiful lovely and pleasant place that's the center of the parliamentary system. Yet, does it merit traveling to? Do you want to include it in your bucket list? If you're a lover of travel and love to travel, then the answer for this question is most definitely positive. In this article, we'll provide some reasons you ought to go. This is a fascinating country interesting, fascinating, bizarre and is awash with stunning gorgeous scenery, making it an amazing country.

While it's small it is likely to be amazed by the variety that it has to offer. There are meadows and hills that are evergreen as well as chalky cliffs, dark, remote mountains that remind you to Emily Bronte and Thomas Hardy as well as other authors. The land boasts stunning national parks as well as possessing some of the most long beaches across Europe.

It is true that England has a plethora of castles and monuments is equally impressive, making it possible to feel the influence of time at each step. There are a mystifying number of castles and fortresses as well as medieval cathedrals and royal palaces dating from the Norman rule. And that isn't the only thing. No matter where you decide to travel, you'll likely be enthralled by the tiny, yet stunning and beautiful countryside.

When to Go to England?

In England is known for its having moody, unpredictable weather. The weather, generally speaking, is uncertain however, in England the weather can turn even more unpredictable. It's okay, so the weather is predictable and you know the kind of weather you can expect and make your travel plans according to the weather. One of the advantages is that you can go to England all year round as the climate is pleasant in the majority of cases.

The peak tourist season for tourists typically occurs during season of summer because temperatures rise the most during the summer season, which makes England attractive during this period. But, as England is an internationally renowned tourist destination, it is a time to see an increase in tourists in comparison to other seasons. The vibe and the energy are what make summer attractive as well as the fact the numerous celebrations and festivals you may like to take part in.

But, if you'd prefer to avoid the crowds and also save money going to the park in the late the season of spring and early autumn could be equally enjoyable. It is a wonderful time to visit and to say the beauty of the landscape is understatement. Actually when it is springtime or fall time, the landscape becomes stunning as it transforms the color.

The weather can be dull and miserable no matter what time of year it is Be ready and wear weather-appropriate clothing as well as waterproof shoes!

Enjoy the Free Museums

If you're a fan of art or simply wish to learn more about the past of our country, it is a must to visit the museums that are free to your benefit. While transportation and accommodation can be expensive in England but you are able to visit the majority of museums for free.

If you're looking forward to visiting the renowned British Museum, the one and only Science Museum or the Natural History Museum located in London You must go, since the cost isn't a cent. But, based on when you're visiting England the crowds may vary from smaller to larger - it's impossible to say you'll know for sure Unfortunately.

Public Transport in England

The public mode of transportation to a new country may be nerve-wracking, especially when it's the first time you've visited the country. When it comes to trains it is important to know it's safe and vast. Therefore, whether you wish to travel through tiny towns or cities, there's a good chance that you'll have the connectivity that you require. If you'd like the best, you can even purchase tickets before you travel. It is possible to reserve tickets twelve weeks before the dates of travel.

If you want to get about in London the simplest and most efficient method of transport is the tube. Tickets can be purchased in stations. There are automated machines at most stations. However, in more crowded ones, there's even vendors. The issue is, that based on how far it is between points A and B, it may take longer to travel there via tube. It is possible to walk between lines particularly in case you need to wait for long periods of period of time. However should you move lines, you must factor in another hour or so in the event that you're exiting Zone One. Zone One.

A further tip is to make sure that you've got an account with a contactless card, you could use it to purchasing tickets. If you're trying to cut down on time and avoid the line to purchase tickets, keep this in mind.

What to See in England?

It is possible to talk for hours about the things to do in England. There is London and is considered to be the heart of England. This is the city that is the best illustration of the evolution of the country through time, and also the way it has risen above a broad variety of obstacles to get what it is today. This is an incredible city however it is quite costly - therefore, you should take this into consideration prior to you go.

If you're more adventurous and would like to live more relaxed, you must consider visiting the coastline. These English coastal towns let the visitor to have a relaxing and slow-moving holiday while giving you the opportunity to take part in a variety of celebrations and events outdoors according to the season of the year when you're there. In addition, Cornwall is also worthy of attention as it's like a miniature New-England or so. Cornwall offers a variety of possibilities to those who are outdoor lover, since the scenery here is stunning.

Also, there is Bath that we've been mentioning before as an example of the impact from Roman Rule in England. You'll be amazed at how well the city has survived many centuries and is still keeping its unique charm and features. If you're planning to visit England in summertime It is essential to put Lake District on your list. Lake District on your list in order to experience the flavor of a truly English summer. But that's not to suggest that the Lake District isn't just as beautiful in spring, or during the autumn

- it depends on the visitor and their preferences to determine the best time for your visit!

Chapter 15: The Rise And Fall Of Roman Britain

When Julius Caesar's first trip to Britain at the time of his visit in 55 BC, Romans had no idea of the distant land there were myths and legends of the terrifying Druids as well as blue-painted wild savages were common within the Roman world. At the end of the 1st century, Britain had been firmly established in the Roman Empire growing into an ever more important and prosperous region that eventually created Roman the emperors it had. The transformation from a fog-filled backwater to this rich expansion of the Empire wasn't smooth sailing. The Iceni staged many rebellions. by Iceni, the Iceni and the Iceni, were commonplace. The brutality of these revolts was so severe that it's difficult to comprehend why Roman rule could not be maintained, but also what was the method by which Romanization proved to be more successful in Britain over the majority of non-Latin provinces in the Empire was accomplished.

The main reasons for this achievement are in the political climate of the island which led to an Roman policy of division and rule. This strategy was employed in conjunction with the traditional strategy of a carrot and stick for peacefully settling what, to the most part would have been unattainable, considering that the Romans had been operating away from their central authority. The Britain conquered by Caesar during the year 55 BCE was inhabited by a vast variety in Iron Age tribes, all belonging to a broad Celtic cultural. Within the situation of Britain However the word "Celtic" must be seen as a term of linguistic origin as, in spite of claims that there were deep-seated cultural connections to Gaul's

Celts from Northern Gaul, there is actually no evidence of the existence of solid ties between Celts within Britain and the Celts of Gaul.

The Brythonic dialect spoken in Britain during this period was comparable to the language is spoken in Ireland as well as Gaul All of which are thought to be Celtic. However, even though the connections among the different centers of Celtic cultural traditions may not have been as extensive as previous scholars believed, it's natural that individuals who have the same language be able to share certain cultural characteristics. Fitzpatrick stated: "It is clear then that there isn't an inherent Celtic European connection and that notions of the concept of a Celtic Iron Age Europe is been developed almost in an random manner. In a critical examination in the context of being Celtic could also be viewed as somewhat formulated."[11 Tacitus believed in the Britons to be the descendants of migrant communities from across Europe. He believed that Caledonians were the descendents of German colonists, whereas those living in Wales were, according to him, originated from Iberia while those to the south were from Gaul: "Their physical characteristics differ and that is in general, however it's plausible to assume that Gauls lived on this island in close proximity to them."[2[2

Researchers have long argued about what the motives behind these movements however whether they were a result of migrations as well as invasions or the result in "diffusion" is largely unimportant. It is important to note that many the tribes of different regions of Europe did eventually settle in Britain and included the Belgae which landed on the island around the second century BCE. Julius Caesar describes this migration in his Commentaries about the Gallic War, using the presumed unity of Belgae and their descendants to justify the invasion of Belgae as well as their ancestors who migrated across the Channel during the battle against Rome to justify the encampment he launched in 55 BCE. [3]

There was a connection between groups within Britain. Evidence from archaeology suggests that, starting in about the time of 8century BCE from the 8th century BCE onwards, Celts in Britain traded with counterparts across the Channel with new ideas in, for example manufacturing swords. Trading was not just limited to the immediate neighbours. In fact, evidence indicates that Phoenician traders started visiting Britain around the same time with a variety of Mediterranean items to bring. In the same way, it's obvious that merchants from Scandinavia transported their goods in Britain. The majority of them were especially interested in Britain's mineral wealth as well as salt. Products were imported from Hallstatt culture, and these specifically affected the art of Britain. Beginning in the 2nd century BCE from the 2nd century BCE onwards, Britons made use of trade routes established by the Romans throughout Brittany and the southwest of France in order to gain access Italian production in addition to Hengistbury Head in Dorset became the hub for importation of Italian wine. [4]

Andreas Wahra's photograph of an old bust of Caesar

Caesar's trips in Britain at the time of 55 BCE as well as 54 BCE need to be seen in context of the political climate within Rome during that period. Caesar was in charge of the vast army of Gaul and his expedition was, to a significant extent, conducted under the basis of battling any external threat to the Empire. The reason for this was his authority over the Gaul army during a period when there was a movement to Rome to have him removed from his position after the conclusion of his term and was planned for the year 54 BCE.

This is why Caesar wanted to keep control of his troops regardless of the cost, and this was essential in his political strategies. In the Gallic Wars, he claimed that the Britons were aiding the Gauls and could pose an extremely real threat to the Roman attempts to calm the new conquered country. 5 The English Channel was generally regarded by the Romans as the absolute limit of space as well as the importance of crossing the "Ocean" was not lost to Caesar and his intent focused on establishing his status as the greatest Roman general as well as a politician.

The first war began at the end of summer 55 BCE, in spite of the reality that it was extremely late in the battle season. Gaius Volusenis was sent in one ship to survey the area of the south coast because Gaulish merchants were refusing to give any details about Britain in order to be able to provide information for Romans. The ship did not arrive, since "he would not abandon his vessel and surrender his life to barbarians."[6The scouting trip was five days long and, with the information that his tribune was able to obtain, Caesar planned his invasion. Many tribes from the southern region of Britain were frightened after they realized the Romans determined to conquer their territory, and many tribes sent envoys of their own to Caesar to offer their acceptance. The emperor sent them back to the island together with his friend the King Commius of the Atrebates and hoped to get all tribes as likely before he arrived.

The fleet of the invasion included 80 vessels of transport capable of transporting Legio VII, Legio X, and other ships. Legio VII as well as the Legio X as well as other battle ships. the entire fleet was based at what's now Boulogne and was then known as Portus Itius. Furthermore, Caesar arranged for a additional 18 transport vessels to transport the cavalry to Ambleteuse following his landing. Seven. The idea that Caesar was certainly in an urgency can be seen in the fact that he embarked just after midnight on the night of August 23rd, 55 BCE not bringing the cavalry along, battle weapons or items he thought were essential for an attempt to conquer. The absence of precise planning is what has caused many historians to conclude Caesar didn't intend for his expedition to be an absolute subjugation.

No matter what the initial goal it's evident that the Romans were originally planning to establish a beachhead at Dover however, upon arriving on the shore, the large numbers of tribal members gathered along the cliffs convinced Caesar to choose discretion as the most important aspect of valor, and so Caesar sailed seven miles further up the coast, to the thought of an unguarded beach, now believed as Pegwell Bay on the Island of Thanet. He then landed. The setting up of a beachhead was extremely challenging, since the British strongly opposed the landings but were only slowed by the ballistae of ships that were anchored near the coast.

Camps were established. Caesar was hostage to the tribes that surrounded him, but the king was unable to establish his bridgehead because the cavalry didn't arrive. Then he realized that he'd no equipment to cope the typical (harsh) British winter. Conscient of the dangers he was in, Caesar decided to return to Gaul instead of risking getting stranded Britain throughout winter and facing the real threat that he would be defeated completely. He was able to return Gaul and continued to take hostages from two tribes in the south-east on the island. However, the other tribes they believed that the threat from Rome was over and opted to ignore their promises.

However this mission is judged--either intended as an invasion, or simply an attempt to gather information, it failed to attain any of its objectives. In spite of this however, the Senate amazed by the realization that Caesar was able to go over what they thought was"the "known world", declared an oath or thanksgiving for twenty days to honor Caesar's achievements.

When he returned in Gaul, Caesar immediately began to prepare for the second assault, set for the year 54 BCE. Cicero mentioned these plans in letters addressed to an acquaintance, requesting for him to ensure that the purchase of an British war chariot. 10. Romans were wiser than their mistakes of 55 BCE and instead of occupying just two Legions at this time the army consisted of five and 22,000 cavalry. All members were transported on vessels specifically designed to be used for landings on beaches. Also, he planned his routes for supplies more precisely and left Labienus in Portus Itius to oversee the daily transportation of essential equipment and food for the operation of an invasion force.

The Romans arrived at the location Caesar recognized earlier in the year, however this time, their landing was uncontested. Once the bridgehead was in place, Caesar ordered Quintus Atrius to move towards the inland. In the course of one day, the force traveled for 12 miles and had defeated the British army within Bigbury Wood. In the following day following day, the Romans set out to advance into the interior, however a devastating storm that destroyed numerous ships of the invasion fleet resulted in Caesar to direct his troops to retreat back to the coasts to make repairs.

In the beginning of September, Caesar was again advancing inland and fought the forces of Cassivellaunus King of the Trinovantes, a tribe located just north of the Thames. Cassivellaunus was the one who had overcame the Trinovantes and now served as the war's leader and also. Together, the Britons were a threat to the Romans but soon realized that they weren't as strong to impose a devastating defeat to the invading forces. Caesar continued to move to the north, but his frequent attack meant that by when he finally arrived at the Thames, the one easily crossed crossing had been strengthened by the Romans who used an elephant in order to intimidate the Britons and the guardsmen into abstaining from the crossing because of terror. 12] The Trinovantes had sent ambassadors to promise aid and provisions to the Cassivellaunus. The

Romans reinstated Mandubraccius to the throne of Trinovantine. Others tribes followed Trinovantine guideline--including the Cenimagni and the Segontiaci and the Ancalites and the Bibroci and the Cassi. They have surrendered. Caesar is with his new, more secure location, occupied Cassivellaunus the last stronghold of Cassivellaunus at Wheathampstead. [13]

Like in the year before, Caesar was eager for an end to the war and feared that he might be left in Britain for the duration of winter. Therefore, he didn't attempt to impose the siege. However, Cassivellaunus offered hostages, tribute, and to not attack the Romans as their new allies the Romans were in agreement with the conditions and left the island. There was no garrison was ever left in Britain for the purpose of enforcing the agreement, and it isn't known whether any tributes were ever due. [14]

Both Caesar's campaigns failed to yield either economic or military advantages however, the second one provided the Romans with an abundance of information about the island which were lacking prior to the wars. Knowledge of the geography was gained not through Roman advance, but rather through conversations with local people. Caesar's findings were restricted to Kent as well as that of the Thames Valley. In his Commentaries regarding the Gallic War,, Caesar made note that "[t]he climate is more temperate than in Gaul the colds being less severe." Also, he wrote "The island has a triangular shape and the sides are opposed to Gaul. A particular angle of the side that is situated in Kent where the majority of ships coming from Gaul are positioned, is towards the east.

Its lower angle looks towards the south. The southern side is around 500 miles. A different side is towards Spain and to the west where the portion of Ireland is less, so it is believed as compared to Britain in one-half and the crossing through it to Britain is the same distance as that to Gaul. The middle of the voyage lies an island that is known as Mona several smaller islands could be found there among which are islands that claim about the fact that on the winter solstice there could remain night for a period of thirty days. In our research on the subject, found nothing other than that, based on precise measurements using water, we could see that nights were longer in the region than those on the continent. The length of this part in this story, according to the account it, is about 700 miles. The third part is towards the north, and to this portion of the island opposes, however this part is primarily towards Germany. The third side is thought as being 800 miles long. The whole island measures around two thousand miles in circumference."[15[15

The total circle of the island considering inlets, and other inlets, is around 11,000 miles. Caesar's estimates of the exact shape of the islands are extremely precise. Being able to evaluate possible landing spots as well as harbors was invaluable during the following century.

Caesar was also able evaluate the Britons as well, forming Roman opinions from then from that point. The historian explained "The Interior of Britain is inhabited by people who claim that they are handed down through traditions to be born on the islands themselves. The sea portion of the island is inhabited by those who crossed through the land of the Belgae in order to plunder and warfare, virtually every one of them is known in the names of those states where they were born. the came and after after having fought war, they returned to the island and then began cultivating the land. There are numerous and the buildings are large for the majority of time much like the ones of Gaul. They don't consider as legal to eat Hare, they do not eat the goose and the cock However, they do cultivate them for pleasure and pleasure."[16[16

Britain didn't officially come to Roman rule until the year 43 CE, during the rule of the Emperor Claudius. However, it should be understood that the whole island never came under the control of Rome and the territory Rome could take on was many generations of work. The result was a regular shift in the boundaries at the border of Rome. This was finally consolidated by the creation of Hadrian's Wall (122-138 CE) and the more recent Antonine Wall (141-158 CE). The Antonine Wall, thought to be was a structure "advance upon Hadrian's turf wall" (Hornblower, Spawforth, and Eidinow) It was the smallest attempt at advancing Rome's frontiers further into contemporary Scotland. The archaeological evidence suggests that there was a "single period of occupation" that lasted from. 139 to 158 CE. The wall was eventually abandoned and razed about 163 CE. (Hornblower, Spawforth, and Eidinow). Then, Hadrian's Wall became rebuilt, and the boundary between the northern Picts of contemporary Scotland as well as the Romans was drawn. The modern-day territory of Scotland has never been "conquered and incorporated into the Roman Empire" (Higham and Ryan 21).

The conquests of Rome that engulfed much of Britain was eventually beginning to produce fruit, which had the point of Tacitus's historian saying that the region was prosperous. But the truth was it proved to be "probably a drain on imperial resources for a century and more" (Higham and Ryan 21). While it was able to produce "highly valued" products such as pearls, hounds and tin, it could be described as "economically marginal" and cost much more to keep than the goods that was available to be purged (Higham and Ryan 22).).

The presence of Rome within Britain was part of what Higham and Ryan refer to as an "frontier society" (22-23). It was evident in the presence of garrisons in local areas all over the countryside, most prominently located in Caerleon, Chester, and York. These garrisons with a settled structure, known as the vici of

Latin (from which comes the suffixes wick and -wich used are used in the names of places such as Warwick and Norwich originate) are "small islands of governmental influence within the wider landscape" of Britain (Higham and Ryan 24). The level of Roman urbanization, which was typical for colonia (colonies) like Londinium (London) is an insignificant minority. The "islands" would have been fascinating mixtures of religions and ethnicities and the legions were drawn all across the Empire (Higham Ryan 25 and Higham Ryan 25) and displayed a style and development style like towns throughout their native American West in the 19th century. Businesses as well as other outcroppings of semi-urbanity emerged from these small cities that were under Roman control (Higham as well as Ryan 23-24). The Roman settlements served as a marker in the line of demarcation between Roman Britain as well as "Celtic" Britain, as "the indigenous population lived in enclosed settlements that changed little in consequence of Roman occupation beyond the appearance of a few pots, small items of metalwork and cheap jewelry" (Higham and Ryan 24). It is apparent that there was a insufficient integration, and growth of Briton traits across other provinces for instance Gaul.

The final Roman Empire has been typically described as a super-state which was smashed and overwhelmed by invaders from abroad, thanks to the seminal, but aged work known as The History of the Decline and Fall of the Roman Empire written by Edward Gibbon. The majority of academics are averse to Gibbon's historic narrative and the perception of the demise of the

Roman Empire. Gibbon's interpretation of the fall is a massive military defeat as well as the destruction of an ancient shining beacon of culture and civilization which led to the creation of a "Dark Age" of barbarity. The majority of historians have firmly abstained from this story in the past few decades. It is now similar to this that the end of the Roman Empire and its collapse (or more precisely, its transformation into smaller states and political systems) resulted from long-winded collapses in the operations of Roman administration and economics, a couple of years into the process of making.

www.ingramcontent.com/pod-product-compliance
Lightning Source LLC
Chambersburg PA
CBHW070555010526
44118CB00012B/1323